Security in the Spirit

Security in the Spirit

by
John MacArthur, Jr.

"GRACE TO YOU"
P.O. Box 4000
Panorama City, CA   91412

©1991 by
JOHN F. MACARTHUR, JR.

All rights reserved. No part of this book may be reproduced in any
form without permission in writing from the publisher, except in the
case of brief quotations embodied in critical articles or reviews.

All Scripture quotations unless noted otherwise, are from the *New
Scofield Reference Bible*, King James Version. Copyright © 1967 by Oxford
University Press, Inc. Reprinted by permission.

Moody Press, a ministry of the Moody Bible Institute, is designed for
education, evangelization, and edification. If we may assist you in
knowing more about Christ and the Christian life, please write us
without obligation: Moody Press, c/o MLM, Chicago, Illinois 60610.

ISBN: 0-8024-5334-1

1 2 3 4 5 Printing/LC/Year 95 94 93 92 91

Printed in the United States of America

Contents

These Bible studies are taken from messages delivered by Pastor-Teacher John MacArthur, Jr., at Grace Community Church in Sun Valley, California. These messages have been combined into a 12-tape album titled *Security in the Spirit*. You may purchase this series either in an attractive vinyl cassette album or as individual cassettes. To purchase these tapes, request the album *Security in the Spirit*, or ask for the tapes by their individual GC numbers. Please consult the current price list; then send your order, making your check payable to:

"GRACE TO YOU"
P.O. Box 4000
Panorama City, CA 91412

Or call the following toll-free number:
1-800-55-GRACE

1

The Spirit Takes Us from Sin to Righteousness

Outline

Introduction
A. The Treasure of Romans
B. The Theme of Romans

Lesson
I. He Frees Us from Sin and Death (vv. 2-3)
II. He Enables Us to Fulfill God's Law (v. 4)
   A. As Depicted in the New Testament
   B. As Depicted in the Old Testament
III. He Changes Our Nature (vv. 5-11)
   A. The Difference Between Our Old and New Natures (vv. 5-6)
      1. Different patterns (v. 5)
      2. Different parallels (v. 6)
   B. The Confines of Our Old Nature (vv. 7-8)
      1. Its inability to submit to God (v. 7)
      2. Its inability to satisfy God (v. 8)
   C. The Implications of Our New Nature (vv. 9-11)
      1. The Spirit's presence proves our salvation (v. 9)
      2. The Spirit's presence guarantees our spiritual regeneration (v. 10)
      3. The Spirit's presence guarantees our physical regeneration (v. 11)

Introduction

Romans 8 brings the ministry of the Holy Spirit to believers into clear focus. Prior to this chapter, the Holy Spirit is mentioned only two other times in the entire epistle (Rom. 1:4; 5:5). But here He is referred to nearly twenty times.

A. The Treasure of Romans

I cannot find words to express all the riches contained in this chapter. As I studied each verse, I felt like I was on an ascending path culminating in a paean of praise. Romans 8 will sweep you off your feet and carry you into the presence of God Himself. When you read such a monumental chapter with an open heart and mind, I guarantee you will be enriched. It would be impossible not to be changed after internalizing the truths contained in this life-changing chapter.

B. The Theme of Romans

Paul has one major theme in Romans: justification by grace through faith based on the Person and work of the Lord Jesus Christ. That is God's plan of salvation. Paul outlines that plan throughout the book of Romans.

In Romans 8:1 Paul says, "There is therefore now no condemnation to them who are in Christ Jesus." We will never be condemned; we will never experience judgment for our sin because we are made righteous in Jesus Christ. That is a marvelous reality, but we will appreciate it only when understanding what it means to be condemned. It's being delivered from the horrors of God's judgment, which are reserved for those who reject Him. As American Puritan Jonathan Edwards alluded to in his famous sermon "Sinners in the Hands of an Angry God," the wrath of God upon the wicked is as intense as His love is to the saints.

The great declaration of no condemnation is so fantastic that Paul uses the rest of the chapter to explain it. In verse 34 he asks the rhetorical question, "Who is he that condemneth?" The obvious answer: No one. The highest court—that of God through Christ—does not condemn us. Therefore, no one else can rightly condemn us.

Many of the Jewish people who listened to Paul would have had a hard time accepting that salvation is by grace through faith alone and not by works. They saw God as a God of wrath. They didn't see how a person could receive freedom from condemnation without good works. Paul wrote Romans 8 to address that issue. There is no

8

condemnation for those in Christ because of what the Holy Spirit does on behalf of believers.

Romans 8 is not an isolated chapter about the Holy Spirit; everything fits within the flow of the book of Romans. Chapters 3-7 detail how Christ frees people from condemnation, and chapter 8 shows how the Holy Spirit confirms that believers face no condemnation.

Lesson

The Holy Spirit does several things to confirm that believers are not condemned: He frees us from sin and death, He enables us to fulfill the law, He changes our nature, He empowers us for victory, He confirms our adoption, and He guarantees our glory. The result of the Holy Spirit's ministry is mentioned in the climactic ending of Romans 8. We can praise God and glory in that tremendous benediction because of what the Spirit does to confirm our no-condemnation status before God.

I. HE FREES US FROM SIN AND DEATH (vv. 2-3)

"The law of the Spirit of life in Christ Jesus hath made me free from the law of sin and death. For what the law could not do, in that it was weak through the flesh, God sending his own Son, in the likeness of sinful flesh and for sin, condemned sin in the flesh."

What is "the law of the Spirit of life"? The gospel, which is a law because it demands our obedience (cf. Acts 17:30). The law of the gospel of life in Christ came to us through the Spirit, and made us free from the law of sin and death. We will never be condemned because we have been set free from the law and its just punishment, which is death (Rom. 6:23). Because of our faith in Christ, the regenerating work of the Spirit has set us free from sin's power and penalty. We will never experience the punishment of sin. What a marvelous truth!

The Holy Spirit is the agent of our salvation. He delivers us out of the dominion of sin, unlocks the chains of transgression, and makes the way of freedom. The Holy Spirit frees us not only from the consequence of our sin, but also from its power so that we need not succumb to it.

9

II.   HE ENABLES US TO FULFILL GOD'S LAW (v. 4)

"The righteousness of the law [is] fulfilled in us, who walk not after the flesh, but after the Spirit."

When a person is saved, he is freed from sin's mastery but not from sin's presence. He will still battle with sin, but it will no longer dominate him because he has the ability to forsake it.

Because a Christian walks "after the Spirit," he is able to fulfill the righteousness of the law. Saint Augustine said, "Grace was given, in order that the law might be fulfilled" (Anti-Pelagian Writings, "On the Spirit and the Letter," chap. 34). When God regenerates a soul, He produces within the person the ability to fulfill God's holy law.

A Christian does not fulfill the law by producing external behavior based on a code of ethics. Holiness, righteousness, and obedience are not external; they are internal. They are the product of the Holy Spirit, who dwells within the believer's heart. When a person becomes a believer, the Holy Spirit takes up residence in him and begins to produce a life of holiness. If a Christian is disobedient, he is fighting against himself and thwarting the Spirit of God. Being a disobedient Christian is like holding your breath—it's easier to do what comes naturally. The disobedient Christian is actually fighting against the new nature within him.

God not only redeemed us transactionally (by imparting Christ's righteousness to us) and forensically (by judicially declaring us righteous), but also planted His Spirit within us to produce the fruit of love, joy, peace, patience, gentleness, goodness, faith, meekness, and self-control (Gal. 5:22-23). That results in actions pleasing to God. Because Christ has given us His Spirit, we can fulfill God's law.

A. As Depicted in the New Testament

   1. Ephesians 2:10—"We are his workmanship, created in Christ Jesus unto good works, which God hath before ordained that we should walk in them." The purpose of redemption is to do good works—to live a holy life.

   2. Titus 2:14—Christ "gave himself for us that he might redeem us from all iniquity, and purify unto himself a people of his own, zealous of good works."

10

3. Hebrews 5:8-9—"Though [Christ] were a Son, yet learned he obedience by the things which he suffered; and being made perfect, he became the author of eternal salvation unto all them that obey him." Those who are saved reflect the obedience and righteousness of the one who saved them.

Justification and sanctification are inseparable truths. If you have been redeemed, you will manifest that reality in your life. You won't be perfect—that won't happen until you are glorified in heaven (1 John 3:2-3)—but the Holy Spirit, who resides in your heart, will produce evidence of a righteousness that fulfills the law.

B. As Depicted in the Old Testament

1. Ezekiel 11:19-20—God gave this promise to the Israelites for the future: "I will give them one heart, and I will put a new spirit within [them]; and I will take the stony heart out of their flesh, and will give them an heart of flesh, that they may walk in my statutes, and keep mine ordinances, and do them." One day God would give His people the Holy Spirit, and His indwelling would enable them to obey His Word.

2. Ezekiel 36:26-27—"A new heart also will I give you, and a new spirit will I put within you; and I will take away the stony heart out of your flesh, and I will give you an heart of flesh. And I will put my Spirit within you, and cause you to walk in my statutes, and ye shall keep mine ordinances, and do them."

III. HE CHANGES OUR NATURE (vv. 5-11)

A. The Differences Between Our Old and New Natures (vv. 5-6)

1. Different patterns (v. 5)

"They that are after the flesh do mind the things of the flesh; but they that are after the Spirit, the things of the Spirit."

There are only two kinds of people in the world: those who follow after the flesh and those who follow after the Spirit. God never divides people by sex, culture, race, class, or education. His concern is whether they follow Him or not.

There are degrees within each category, however. Some Christians don't mind the things of the Spirit as well as they ought to. Some who mind the things of the flesh actually behave better than some Christians. Yet despite the degrees within each category, the categories themselves are absolute. David Brown, commenting on Romans 8:5, said, "Men must be under the predominating influence of one or other of these two principles, and, according as the one or the other has the mastery, will be the complexion of their life, the character of their actions" (Robert Jamieson and A. R. Fausset, *A Commentary, Critical and Explanatory, on the Old and New Testaments* [Grand Rapids: Zondervan, 1945], vol. 2, p. 240). Then, quoting commentator Charles Hodge, he continued, "The bent of the thoughts, affections, and pursuits, is the only decisive test of character" (p. 241).

People who walk after the Spirit do so because they think about the things of the Spirit and live their lives according to the Spirit. Those who walk in the flesh have their minds on the things of the flesh because they live according to the flesh. Romans 8:8-9 indicates that the those who are after the flesh are in the flesh. Their fleshly nature causes them to have fleshly thinking patterns (or a fleshly disposition), which becomes manifest in their behavior. A Christian is able to fulfill God's law because he has proper thinking patterns, which come from his new nature. From the moment of his conversion, a Christian's disposition is changed toward the things of the Spirit.

a) Those who are dominated by the flesh

The phrase "they that are after the flesh" (v. 5) in the Greek text literally says "the ones being according to the flesh." An unsaved person is dominated by his depraved, unredeemed flesh. To be "after the flesh" is the same as being "in the flesh" (v. 8). "After the flesh" emphasizes the determining pattern; "in the flesh" emphasizes the conditioning sphere. Both phrases refer to people dominated by human corruption.

When a person is "after the flesh," he will "mind the things of the flesh" (v. 5). The common Greek word translated "mind" (*nous*) refers to the brain and its function, but here Paul used *phroneō*, which means "disposition" or "bent." It is derived from the root word *phrēn*, which refers to the seat of all mental affections and faculties. Unbelieving people are disposed toward the things of the flesh. First John 2:15-16 says that if a person has a love or bent toward the world, he is not of God. *Phroneō* is also used in Philippians 2:5, which says, "Let this mind be in you, which was also in Christ Jesus." Our Lord was bent toward humbly submitting to God, and we are to follow His example.

Those who mind the things of the flesh are bent toward depravity. Their minds are not set on God but on all that's temporal and corrupt in this world (cf. Rom. 1:28-31; Gal. 5:19-21). Fleshly things have no connection with the eternal kingdom of God.

All unredeemed people are in the flesh. Since they are fleshly by nature, they are bent toward the things of the flesh.

b) Those dominated by the Spirit

In contrast, Romans 8:5 speaks of "they that are after the Spirit, [who mind] the things of the Spirit." Since the Holy Spirit dwells in those who are redeemed, they are bent toward the things of the Spirit. They walk in the Spirit and pursue what is precious to him. That's why Paul said, "I delight in the law of God after the inward man" (Rom. 7:22). Now what are the things of the Spirit? First Corinthians 2:10 says, "The Spirit searcheth all things, yea, the deep things of God." That encompasses the very mind and will of God.

The phrases "mind the things of the flesh" and "[mind] the things of the Spirit" in Romans 8:5 are genitives of possession. An unregenerate person's mind is possessed by the flesh and a regenerate person's mind is controlled by the Spirit. We who have been redeemed have been given a new nature. We are no longer walking after the things of the flesh; we are now walking in the direction of God's Spirit.

2. Different parallels (v. 6)

"To be carnally minded is death, but to be spiritually minded is life and peace."

Verse 6 gives us a deeper distinction between those who are after the flesh and those who are after the Spirit. Notice it doesn't say that to be fleshly minded *leads* to death or to be spiritually minded *leads* to life. Rather, to be fleshly minded *is* death and to be spiritually minded *is* life and peace. Those are equations, not consequences.

a) Death for the carnal

The person who does not know God and is bent toward the flesh is spiritually dead. Ephesians 2:1 says, "You hath he made alive, who were dead in trespasses and sins." First Timothy 5:6 says, "She that liveth in pleasure is dead while she liveth." A carnally minded person is spiritually dead—the life of God is absent in his soul. He lives physically but not spiritually.

Romans 7:5 says, "When we were in the flesh, the sinful impulses, which were by the law, did work in our members to bring forth fruit unto death." Sin is so dominant in unregenerate people that all it produces is death. Men and women without the Lord live in a state of death.

b) Life and peace for the spiritual

"To be spiritually minded is life and peace," however (Rom. 8:6). When God's Spirit changes a person's nature, He makes him alive to God and spiritual truth. First Corinthians 2:14 says, "The natural man receiveth not the things of the Spirit of God." However, the Holy Spirit enables a redeemed person to understand spiritual things (1 Cor. 2:15-16).

When we were redeemed, we were given new life. Romans 6:4 says that since we died with Christ, we will also rise with Him. If we were buried with Him in His death, we will rise with Him in His resurrection, and walk in newness of life. The Spirit of God has made us alive to God. Because we have

14

new life we who are redeemed can feel God's love, sense His power, and understand His Word and work in our lives.

A person who is spiritually minded also has peace with God. Before a person is saved, he is at war with God. But after redemption, God becomes his constant companion.

We who are redeemed have life. In that life we have sweet communion with God. His grace is bestowed upon us, and His love is shed abroad in our hearts (Rom. 5:5). We have joy forever and are at peace with Him for eternity.

Why Do Believers Still Sin After They Are Saved?

Even though we are redeemed, we don't always pursue the things of the Spirit. Before we were redeemed, however, we never pursued them. Galatians 5:17 says, "The flesh lusteth against the Spirit, and the Spirit against the flesh; and these are contrary the one to the other, so that ye cannot do the things that ye would." Even though we were given new life when we were redeemed, sin is still in us, though it doesn't dominate us anymore (Rom. 7:17-18). When we are glorified, we will no longer be in the flesh, but for now we have to battle against it.

An unsaved person doesn't battle against sin because he is disposed toward it and dominated by it. A Christian has to battle against it because he is indwelt by the Spirit of God, and the flesh strives against the Spirit (Gal. 5:17). Galatians 5:16 tells us how to win the battle: "Walk in the Spirit, and ye shall not fulfill the lust of the flesh." We have to respond to the Spirit and not to the flesh. The latter produces the sins mentioned in verses 19-21, and the Spirit produces the virtues listed in verses 22-23. Verse 25 concludes, "If we live in the Spirit, let us also walk in the Spirit." The Spirit-filled life is a step-by-step journey. Those of us who are redeemed will always struggle with our humanness until the time God perfects us.

B. The Confines of Our Old Nature (vv. 7-8)

1. Its inability to submit to God (v. 7)

"The carnal mind is enmity against God; for it is not subject to the law of God, neither, indeed, can be."

a) In unbelievers

A depraved person cannot subject himself to the law of God. That's because he is at war with God and dead spiritually, for he is cut off from God, who is the source of life. However, a person who minds the things of the Spirit is able to have victory over his sins through the Spirit's power.

The Greek word translated "mind" in verse 7 is also *phroneō*, so the text literally says, "The fleshly mind is bent against God." That's why an unbeliever doesn't obey the law of God. His bent against God is seated deeper than mere disobedience: an unbeliever's acts of disobedience are just the external manifestations of the mind's disposition. Sin is not only outward rebellion, but also an inward attitude. There is no way that the flesh can be subject to the law of God.

b) In believers

You might ask, "Since I have been redeemed, is my flesh now subject to the law of God?" No, because your flesh has not yet been redeemed. If it had been when you were saved, you would be perfect. But you are not because you still have unredeemed flesh to contend with. That's why salvation has a future aspect. Romans 8:23 says, "We ourselves groan within ourselves, waiting for the adoption, that is, the redemption of our body."

Since our humanness cannot fulfill the law of God, it has to be eliminated. But that won't happen until we receive our glorified bodies in heaven.

When you are redeemed, you become a new creation (2 Cor. 5:17). But you are still in your mortal body, which cannot be redeemed in this life. That's why Paul called it "the body of this death" (Rom. 7:24).

2. Its inability to satisfy God (v. 8)

"So, then, they that are in the flesh cannot please God."

Depraved people cannot please God because they cannot obey Him. That's tragic because God created mankind to please Him. The *summum bonum* of all creation is to be to the praise of His glory (Eph. 1:12). Those who don't please God have forfeited their reason for existence.

C. The Implications of Our New Nature (vv. 9-11)

1. The Spirit's presence proves our salvation (v. 9)

"Ye are not in the flesh but in the Spirit, if so be that the Spirit of God dwell in you. Now if any man have not the Spirit of Christ, he is none of his."

In verses 5-8 Paul refers to "they"; but here in verse 9 he says "ye" because he is speaking to believers only. Believers are neither in the flesh nor bent toward it. Far from being opposed to God, we are able to fulfill His law and please Him. We are in the Spirit, who has given us a new nature. John 3:6 says, "That which is born of the flesh is flesh; and that which is born of the Spirit is spirit." A Christian is born of the Spirit and is no longer in the flesh. Although the flesh is still in him, it isn't controlling his life.

If the Spirit dwells in you, then you are not in the flesh but in the Spirit. Being in the Spirit is not a matter of professing Christ, looking holy, or attending church, but of being indwelt by the Spirit. The Greek word translated "dwell" (*oikeō*) indicates that the Spirit makes His home in you. He lives in every believer. However, he who doesn't have the Holy Spirit residing within him doesn't belong to Christ.

People need to be warned about that. If your life isn't showing evidence of the power and presence of God's Spirit, then you don't belong to Christ. If you aren't fulfilling God's righteous law, desiring to walk in the way of the Spirit, and seeking with your heart the things of the Spirit, then He is not in you. No matter what you claim, you don't belong to Christ.

We are all called to examine ourselves. Second Corinthians 13:5 says, "Examine yourselves, whether you are in the faith." Look for manifestations of the Holy Spirit in your life. Have you experienced a divine sense of love, joy, peace, gentleness, goodness, faith,

17

meekness, and self-control (Gal. 5:22-23)? Do you see the fruit of righteousness in your life? Do you long to commune with the living God? Have you ever had a love for God's Word? Does your heart praise God? If you have experienced those things in your life, know that they were produced by the Spirit. Even though you may behave in a fleshly way occasionally, if those things have generally characterized your life, the Spirit of God obviously dwells within you.

All Christians struggle with sin. Paul said that sin dwelt within him (Rom. 7:17, 20). However, it's comforting to know that the Spirit also dwells within us.

The Perfect Trinitarian Balance

Romans 8:9 refers to the Holy Spirit as both "the Spirit of God" and "the Spirit of Christ." The Holy Spirit sustains the same relationship with the Father that He has with the Son. There is a perfect trinitarian balance. The Holy Spirit stands alone as the third Person of the Trinity. He is the Spirit of God (who is the first Person of the Trinity) and the Spirit of Christ (the second Person of the Trinity).

2. The Spirit's presence guarantees our spiritual regeneration (v. 10)

"If Christ be in you, the body is dead because of sin, but the Spirit is life because of righteousness."

When a person receives the indwelling Christ, his body remains the prey of death because the flesh doesn't get redeemed in this life. That's why Christians still have to face death. The body must be eliminated because it can't go to heaven. What about those who will be raptured before the Lord's return (1 Thess. 4:13-17)? Will their bodies to heaven? No, they will be changed on the way. God will not let any unredeemed bodies into heaven. The body of death will die—it is stained with Adam's sin. It will suffer from disease, sickness, and trials. Eventually it will weaken and die. But "the Spirit"—the Holy Spirit and your human spirit with its new nature—will live because of Christ's righteousness. Bodily death is the result of Adam's sin (Rom. 5:12). Like the rest of humanity, you entered the world as a sinner. But because Christ now lives within you, death will merely usher you into eternity. And we won't take the bodies we have up into heaven; we'll get new bodies (1 Cor. 15:44-53). In Philippians 3:8-9 Paul joyfully says, "I count all things but loss . . . that I may win Christ, and be found in him, not having my own righteousness . . . but that which is through the faith of Christ, the righteousness which is of God by faith."

3. The Spirit's presence guarantees our physical regeneration (v. 11)

"If the Spirit of him that raised up Jesus from the dead dwell in you, he that raised up Christ from the dead shall also give life to your mortal bodies by his Spirit that dwelleth in you."

If the Holy Spirit dwells in you, you have the assurance that the Father will raise you from the dead just as certainly as He raised Christ. God promises you a glorified body. If you were regenerated spiritually, you will be regenerated physically as well.

What does the Holy Spirit do for us? He takes us from sin to righteousness by freeing us from sin and death, enabling us to fulfill God's law and changing our nature so that we become new inside and out.

Focusing on the Facts

1. What is the major theme of the book of Romans (see p. 8)?
2. What is "the law of the Spirit of life" (Rom. 8:2)? Explain. Why can we never be condemned (see p. 9)?
3. Explain a saved person's relationship to sin (see p. 10).
4. How does a believer fulfill God's law? What is a believer doing when he is disobedient (see p. 10)?
5. What is the relationship between justification and sanctification (see p. 11)?
6. What are the only two kinds of people in the world from God's perspective (see pp. 11-12)?
7. In Romans 8:5 what do the phrases "after the flesh," "in the flesh," and "mind the things of the flesh" refer to (see pp. 12-13)?
8. What are the "things of the flesh" (see p. 13)?
9. What is true about a carnally minded person? What do spiritually minded people have (Rom. 8:6; see p. 14)?

10. Why do Christians have to battle with sin? Do non-Christians person have to battle against sin? Explain (see p. 15).
11. How can we win our battle against sin (Gal. 5:16; see p. 15)?
12. Can the fleshly mind submit to God (Rom. 8:7)? Explain (see pp. 15-16).
13. Why are we not perfect at the moment of salvation (see p. 16)?
14. Why is it tragic that unredeemed people cannot please God (see p. 17)?
15. How will the Holy Spirit be manifested in a believer's life (see p. 17)?
16. Why do Christians have to die? What will keep our spirits alive for eternity (Rom. 8:10; see pp. 18-19)?
17. What great promise is made in Romans 8:11 (see p. 19)?

Pondering the Principles

1. In Romans 8:1 Paul says, "There is . . . no condemnation to them who are in Christ Jesus." Sometimes it's easy for believers to overlook the fact that God will not punish them for their sins. Read the following verses and describe what it would be like to be subject to God's wrath: Matthew 13:40-42; Romans 2:5-9; 2 Thessalonians 1:7-9; and Revelation 6:15-17; 20:11-15. How would you feel if you knew you had to endure endless years of torment and darkness? Thank God for sparing you from His wrath as a result of the righteousness that Christ provided for you.

2. When you were saved, the Holy Spirit freed you from the law of sin and death. Read Romans 6. Before you became a Christian, what were you a servant to (vv. 17-22)? As a Christian, what is your current relationship to sin (vv. 1-2, 6-7, 11-15)? How then should you live your life (vv. 4, 11-13, 18-19, 22)? Those verses all indicate that you do not need to succumb to sin, because the Holy Spirit has enabled you to live righteously. Prayerfully examine yourself now to make sure that your desire to live righteously for God is stronger than your desire to give in to sin.

3. Romans 8:8 says that those who "are in the flesh cannot please God." However, if you are a Christian, one of the goals in your life should be to please God. Read Romans 12:1-2; 14:17-18; 2 Corinthians 5:9; Ephesians 5:5-10; and 1 Thessalonians 4:1. What is associated with pleasing God? Do you make a conscious effort to please God in all that you do? Make a list of the things you are doing now that please

God. Are there other things you could or should do to please Him? Add those things onto your list and begin to do them this week.

4. Romans 8:11 says that if the Holy Spirit dwells in you, the Father will give life to your mortal body. One of the greatest promises that God has given in Scripture is that someday we will receive new, glorified bodies. Read 1 Corinthians 15:49-53; Philippians 3:20-21; and 1 John 3:2-3. What do those verses say about our future bodily resurrection? It is easy for us to be distracted by the routines and problems of everyday life, and forget the wonderful things that God has promised for our future. Thank God for His promise to regenerate your physical body.

2

The Spirit Empowers Us for Victory

Outline

Introduction

Review

Lesson
I.   The Means of Achieving Victory
     A. Using the Weapons of the Spirit
     B. Walking in the Spirit
     C. Being Filled with the Spirit
II. The People Who Experience Victory
III. The Privilege of Victory
     A. Identifying the Privilege
     B. Ignoring the Privilege
IV. The Pattern for Victory
     A. Stated
        1. Don't live according to the flesh
        2. Live according to the Spirit
     B. Specified
        1. Recognize the presence of sin in your flesh
        2. Fix your heart on God
        3. Meditate on God's Word
        4. Pray diligently
        5. Have a passion to obey God
     C. Sustained
V.   Our Gratitude for Victory

Introduction

Only God has the capability to fill our life with song. Only He
can save and redeem us. As a result we owe Him a tremen-

dous debt. That's why Paul said, "Therefore, brethren, we are debtors, not to the flesh, to live after the flesh. For if ye live after the flesh, ye shall die; but if ye, through the Spirit, do mortify the deeds of the body, ye shall live" (Rom. 8:12-13).

Review

The Holy Spirit does several things to prove that we as believers will never be condemned for our sin: He frees us from sin and death (Rom. 8:2-3; see p. 9), enables us to fulfill God's law (v. 4; see pp. 10-11), and changes our nature (vv. 5-11; see pp. 11-19). We are not under condemnation because we have been made new: the Spirit of God regenerates us spiritually. Verse 11 promises us that someday He will also regenerate us physically.

Lesson

Verses 12-13 tell us that the Holy Spirit also empowers us for victory over the flesh. That's similar to His enabling us to fulfill God's law, but it doesn't focus as much on what the Holy Spirit does for us as on what we do as we allow the Holy Spirit to accomplish His work in us. That's indicated by the phrases "*we* are debtors" and "[*we* must] mortify the deeds of the body." God calls us to deal with sin in our lives, and He never asks us to do something He doesn't enable us to do—that would be futile.

I. THE MEANS OF ACHIEVING VICTORY

If we are going to achieve victory over sin, it will be through the power of the Holy Spirit (v. 13). If we didn't have the Spirit's supernatural power in our lives, we would be unable to overcome the flesh—to kill sin—because the flesh can't overcome flesh. Sin can't gain victory over sin. We must be transformed first (vv. 5-11). Once we have within us the life of God in the presence of His indwelling Spirit, we have power to overcome the flesh. In Romans 7:18 Paul says, "I know that in me (that is, in my flesh) dwelleth no good thing; for to will is present with me, but how to perform that which is good I find not." Paul recognized that apart from God, there was within himself no resource for doing good. That's true for all of us—we have no capacity to gain victory over the flesh on our own.

Romans 8:5-8 says, "They that are after the flesh do mind the things of the flesh. . . . The carnal mind is enmity against God; for it is not subject to the law of God, neither, indeed, can be. So, then, they that are in the flesh cannot please God." Apart from the Holy Spirit's power, a person is controlled by a debilitating corruption. An unregenerate person has no capacity to deal with sin in a manner pleasing to God. But when the Spirit enters a person's life, that changes. With His presence comes the capacity to overcome the flesh.

A. Using the Weapons of the Spirit

    1. 2 Corinthians 10:1-5—"I, Paul, myself beseech you by the meekness and gentleness of Christ, who in presence am base among you, but being absent am bold toward you—but I beseech you, that I may not be bold when I am present with that confidence, with which I think to be bold against some, who think of us as if we walked according to the flesh. For though we walk in the flesh, we do not war after the flesh (for the weapons of our warfare are not carnal, but mighty through God to the pulling down of strongholds)" (vv. 1-4). We are not superhuman; we live in fleshly bodies. But God has given us powerful weapons to fight against sin, and they are available through the power of the Holy Spirit.

    Those weapons are able to cast down "imaginations, and every high thing that exalteth itself against the knowledge of God, and [bring] into captivity every thought to the obedience of Christ" (v. 5). Paul did not conduct himself according to the flesh. Even though he lived in a human body, he fought with spiritual weapons.

    2. Romans 7:24-25—Verses 14-23 chronicle Paul's struggle to do what was right. In verse 24 he laments, "Oh, wretched man that I am! Who shall deliver me from the body of this death?" Paul suffered tremendous anxiety because he loved God's truth and wanted to obey God. Yet he found within himself a power that held him back. He summed up his struggle in verse 25: "With the mind I myself serve the law of God; but with the flesh, the law of sin." We all experience that same struggle. But our anxiety will be resolved when we realize we can have victory over the flesh because

25

we have weapons that are not fleshly but mighty and spiritual.

B. Walking in the Spirit

Galatians 5:17 says, "The flesh lusteth against the Spirit, and the Spirit against the flesh; and these are contrary the one to the other, so that ye cannot do the things that ye would." The flesh and the Spirit battle against each other. But verses 24-25 tell us how to resolve that battle: "They that are Christ's have crucified the flesh with the affections and lusts. If we live in the Spirit, let us also walk in the Spirit." The battle is resolved as we walk in the power of the Holy Spirit.

When you became a Christian, the Spirit of God entered into your life. With Him came the power of God, which is mighty enough to tear down anything that exalts itself against God. You have an internal resource that enables you to have victory over Satan, demons, and the flesh so that you can bring everything in your life into obedience to Christ.

Even You Can Be Perfect!

This may shock you, but you actually have the potential to be perfect. Now in this life you won't always experience victory over sin, but that's not because you don't have the power for victory, but because you don't appropriate it. Your potential to be perfect is debilitated by the power of the flesh. Nevertheless, it is still there. The Greek word translated "power" in the New Testament is *dunamis,* from which we get "dynamite." The power of God is like dynamite in your life!

C. Being Filled with the Spirit

The key to victory is appropriating the power you already have. Ephesians 5:18 says, "Be not drunk with wine, in which is excess [Gk., *asōtia,* "dissipation"], but be filled with the Spirit." That means you must continuously allow the Holy Spirit to permeate your life: you think His thoughts, feel His feelings, and obey His will.

When you are filled with the Spirit, you are controlled by Him. A person is controlled by whatever fills his mind. An adage referring to computers says, "Garbage in,

26

garbage out." Likewise, whatever you put into your mind is going to control your behavior. If you let the Spirit of God control your mind, it will be renewed in the Spirit and you will manifest godly behavior.

"Be filled with the Spirit" is not a command to fall into a trance or have an ecstatic experience; it simply means you are to allow your life to be controlled by the Spirit. The Greek word translated "filled" (*plēroō*) is often used in the gospels about being filled with a particular attitude or feeling, such as hate, bitterness, or rage. When a person is filled with hate, he is dominated by it. Most of the time we maintain an equilibrium between anger and happiness. But once we become filled with anger, we lose our equilibrium and become totally controlled by that emotion. Similarly, a Christian is to be totally under the control of the Spirit.

Ephesians 5:19-21 lists the results of being filled with the Spirit: "Speaking to yourselves in psalms and hymns and spiritual songs, singing and making melody in your heart to the Lord, giving thanks always for all things . . . submitting yourselves one to another." Every relationship you have will be affected when you are filled with the Spirit (Eph. 5:2–16:9).

Colossians 3 is a parallel, condensed version of Ephesians 5:18–6:9. Verse 16 says, "Let the word of Christ dwell in you richly." Notice that the results are the same as those from being filled with the Spirit. You will speak in psalms, hymns, and spiritual songs (v. 16); give thanks (v. 17); and relationships among husbands and wives (vv. 18-19), children and parents (vv. 20-21), and servants and masters (3:22–4:1) will be positively affected. The only apparent difference between Colossians 3:16–4:1 and Ephesians 5:18–6:9 is what produces the results. If you get the same results from letting "the word of Christ dwell in you" as you do when you are "filled with the Spirit," they both must be the same thing.

If you want to live a Spirit-filled life, don't look for ecstatic experiences. Rather, align your life under the Word of God. As you saturate your heart, soul, and mind with God's truth, you will manifest Spirit-controlled behavior. That's why studying God's precious truth is such a great priority. When you are saturated with God's Word, your involuntary responses will be godly—no matter what may happen to you. Now it's comparatively easy to

27

control your voluntary responses. You may think, *I want to be careful how I react in this situation. I want others to think I'm spiritual.* But if someone were to slam you against a wall, you wouldn't have time to think about your reaction. Therefore, you want your involuntary responses to be godly. Living a Spirit-filled life requires a day-by-day awareness of God's Word. You need to meditate on it and let it control your thinking and behavior.

You have the power to kill sin because of the Spirit's presence in you. Don't think you can't overcome sin. The Holy Spirit's power is in you, and you need to appropriate it.

II. THE PEOPLE WHO EXPERIENCE VICTORY

Romans 8:12 says, "Brethren, we are debtors." The people who experience victory over sin are those who know and love the Lord. Unbelievers will never know victory. They may be involved in a religious system that gives them superficial piety on the outside, but they will never know ultimate victory over the flesh. Some immoral people want to feel better about themselves, so they act morally; others don't care about appearing moral. But it's not the presence or absence of morality that ultimately has anything to do with eternal life; it is whether a person knows God through Jesus Christ.

The residual image of God in people makes them want to be moral. Even the most immoral unbelievers want to escape from their problems, but they don't know how. The mental institutions and hospitals of our country are filled with people who are sick of their internal debilitation. They can't have meaningful relationships, nor can they adapt to their circumstances with a sense of true joy. Only those who are in God's family can experience victory over the corruption of the flesh.

III. THE PRIVILEGE OF VICTORY

A. Identifying the Privilege

The first word in verse 12 is "therefore." That's significant because it indicates a point is about to be made from what was previously said. Because we have been delivered from sin and death and enjoy the blessings of righteousness in Christ, a new nature, spiritual giftedness,

28

hope, joy, peace, love, and everything else we have in Christ, we are therefore debtors to God.

All New Testament exhortation is based on privilege. For example, in Romans 12:1 Paul says, "I beseech you therefore, brethren, by the mercies of God, that ye present your bodies a living sacrifice." Based on God's mercy, which Paul examined in the first eleven chapters of Romans, he implored believers to make the necessary sacrifices in serving God. In the first three chapters of Ephesians, Paul expounds on the privileges of being a Christian. Then he says, "I, therefore, the prisoner of the Lord, beseech you that ye walk worthy" (4:1). After discussing our Christian privileges in the first four chapters of Galatians, Paul says, "Stand fast, therefore, in the liberty with which Christ hath made us free, and be not entangled again with the yoke of bondage" (5:1). Because of what Christ has done for us, we are privileged to be able to respond to Him.

Exhortation is always based on an understanding of privilege. We must know what God has done for us before we can understand why we should obey. We can't just browbeat people into submitting to God's laws without telling them what God has done for them.

B. Ignoring the Privilege

When the Israelites were about to enter the Promised Land, they sent ten spies to investigate. When they returned, most of them had what I call the Grasshopper Complex: they saw the people in the land as if they were giants and themselves as grasshoppers in comparison. They didn't believe they could conquer them with or without God's help (Num. 13:33). But Caleb said that God promised to deliver the land to them, and that they should take it (v. 30). Some of us are like the Israelites: God has given us promises, but we don't act on them. We need to remember the power and privileges we have as God's people and claim the promises that He has given us.

IV. THE PATTERN FOR VICTORY

Romans 8:13 says, "If ye live after the flesh, ye shall die; but if ye, through the Spirit, do mortify the deeds of the body, ye shall live."

A. Stated

1. Don't live according to the flesh

The pattern for victory is not to live "after the flesh." We owe nothing to it. What did it ever do for us? Nothing good.

As Christians we are not in the flesh but in the Spirit. And Romans 8:5 says, "They that are after the flesh do mind the things of the flesh; but they that are after the Spirit, the things of the Spirit." If you are not fleshly, why would you want to act fleshly? It would be ridiculous for you to say, "I'm not a murderer, but I enjoy acting like one," or, "I'm not a homosexual, but I like to act like it." Why would you want to act like something you are not?

The flesh is the ugly complex of fallen human desires. It involves motive, affection, principle, purpose, and everything else that evil generates within you. To live after the flesh means to be ruled by it. Since you, as a believer, walk in the Spirit, it would be contradictory for you to think you owe something to the flesh. You have been freed from sin and death. You have been made a new creation and need not live according to the flesh any longer.

a) The reason

Romans 8:13 states, "If ye live after the flesh, ye shall die." Verse 6 likewise says, "To be carnally minded is death." People who are without Christ are spiritually dead and are headed toward eternal death. They mind the things of the flesh and walk in the flesh. They are unable to please God and will be eternally separated from Him. There is no reason for you to act like an unbeliever.

Romans 8:12-13 is one of many self-examination passages in Scripture. Such passages call us to look at our lives to determine if we are saved. The person who is habitually dominated by his sin nature is unsaved and spiritually dead. Someone said to me, "There's a man I know who says he's a Christian, but I don't believe him. He has no desire for the things of the Lord and habitually seeks the things of the flesh." I replied, "That man's claim is meaningless by the test of Scripture. If a person lives after the flesh, he gives evidence that he is on the way to eternal death." No Christian can live like that. Ephesians 2:10 says we were "created in Christ Jesus unto good works."

b) The relapse

Can a Christian ever do something fleshly? Yes. There will be times when a believer will lapse into bad behavior. Paul said, "I, brethren, could not speak unto you as unto spiritual, but as unto carnal. . . . Ye are yet carnal; for whereas there is among you envying, and strife, and divisions . . . " (1 Cor. 3:1-3). In Romans 7 Paul gives a personal account of the battle all Christians have with sin—sometimes we win; sometimes we lose. But the primary disposition of a believer is toward the things of the Spirit.

c) The resolve

Paul stated his resolve to live like Christ this way: "[I want to] be found in him, not having mine own righteousness . . . but that which is through the faith of Christ . . . that I may know him, and the power of his resurrection, and the fellowship of his sufferings" (Phil. 3:9-10). Paul wanted to know Christ, His resurrection power, and His sufferings to the fullest extent. Nevertheless, he didn't want to presume that he was already perfect (v. 12).

Paul knew he was saved by grace but also wanted to live out his salvation with all his heart. He refused to let his flesh hold him back. In verses 13-14 he says, "I count not myself to have apprehended; but this one thing I do, forgetting those things which are behind, and reaching forth unto those things which are before, I press toward the mark for the prize of the high calling of God in Christ Jesus."

Paul had a tremendous passion to know God, enjoy fellowship with Christ, and use all the power available to him. That was the bent of his life, even though there were times when he was interrupted in that pursuit by his flesh. Every Christian who seeks the things of God will struggle with sin. But if you live habitually after the flesh, you give evidence of being on your way to eternal death. The presence of holiness is absolutely necessary for any Christian.

The pattern for victory is to owe nothing to the flesh. As Paul said, "Shall we continue in sin, that grace may abound? God forbid. How shall we, that are dead to sin, live any longer in it? . . . We are buried with [Christ] by baptism into death, that as [He] was raised up from the dead by the glory of the Father, even so we also should walk in newness of life" (Rom. 6:1-4).

2. Live according to the Spirit

In Romans 8:13 Paul says, "If ye, through the Spirit, do mortify the deeds of the body, ye shall live." That is a fact. It is valid to examine a person's salvation on the basis of his or her behavior. You can look at salvation from two perspectives: God's sovereignty and the individual's behavior. Here Paul speaks from the perspective of behavior.

a) Pursue the Spirit

It is characteristic of a Christian to pursue the things of the Spirit and kill the deeds of the flesh. There will be times when he fails to do that, but generally he desires the things of God and to remove sin from his life. Righteous living assures a believer of his salvation. No other argument for his security is as convincing as having victory over sin (2 Pet. 1:5-10). You can be sure you're a Christian in two ways: by believing God's Word that your faith in Christ is what saves you (cf. Rom. 10:9-10) and by experiencing victory over sin.

b) Purge sin

Romans 8:13 says we must kill the deeds of the body. The body represents our flesh. Sin tempts us through the body—through our eyes and ears. Throughout Romans 6 and 7 Paul refers to the flesh and the body of sin. Our sin is in our flesh, and our minds and feelings are a part of our flesh. We should constantly be killing the deeds of the flesh through the Spirit's power.

The Greek word translated "mortify" in Romans 8:13 is used in 1 Peter 3:18 to refer to Christ's death. We are to kill sin by the power of the Spirit. When God told King Saul to destroy the Amalekites, he disobeyed by sparing their king and some animals (1 Sam. 15:2-23). We're not to do that with sin—we must kill it for sure. We must not leave any bleating sheep in our lives to betray our disobedience (1 Sam. 15:14). Many Christians retain certain sins in their lives because they don't want to kill them.

Colossians 3 says, "If ye, then, be risen with Christ, seek those things which are above, where Christ sitteth on the right hand of God. Set your affection on things above, not on things on the earth. For ye are dead, and your life is hidden with Christ in God. . . . Mortify [kill], therefore, your members which are upon the earth: fornication, uncleanness, inordinate affection, evil desire, and covetousness. . . . But now ye also put off all these: anger, wrath, malice, blasphemy, filthy communication out of your mouth. Lie not one to another, seeing that ye have put off the old man with his deeds" (vv. 1-9). If you belong to Christ, you must seek out and destroy the residual sins that are in you.

When you came to Christ and had your sins forgiven, your responsibility to kill off sin began. You will spend the rest of your life doing that. It will be difficult—just when you think you've conquered a problem, it will pop up again. However, some give the impression that it's easy. I call them the "deeper-life people." They appear as if they've ascended to a level where conflict with sin never occurs. That's impossible in this life because sin is always at work in the human heart. Don't be fooled when it appears as if you've wiped out sin in your life.

Puritan John Owen warned that sin is never less quiet than when it seems to be most quiet, and its waters are for the most part deep, when they are still (cf. *Sin & Temptation* [Portland: Multnomah, 1983], p. xxi). Sin would love to lull you into thinking you're OK. Although you may not steal, murder, or commit fornication, if you don't deal with anger, bitterness, and ill will in your life, you won't experience true victory. Your battle with sin will go on as long as you live, but you can experience victory.

B. Specified

Don't let anyone tell you he or she has reached complete consecration. Anyone who claims that is self-deceived (1 John 1:8). Practical sanctification will continue as long as we live. The following are some practical ways to kill sin in your life.

1. Recognize the presence of sin in your flesh

The apostle Paul admitted, "I find then a law, that, when I would do good, evil is present with me" (Rom. 7:21). Even if you are a pastor, deacon, elder, or a Bible study teacher, don't live under the illusion that sin isn't in your life. Paul said of himself, "Oh, wretched man that I am!" (v. 24). You will never know victory over sin until you recognize its presence in your life.

You have to know your enemy before you can kill it. How sad that many of us never search out the poison in our lives. We seldom look at the Word of God, meditate, and pray over it, asking, "God, search me and know my heart" (cf. Ps. 139:23-24). In that psalm David is asking God to let him see the corruption in him so he could fight it. We, on the other hand, tend to allow sin to camouflage itself. We'll shrug it off by claiming to have a weakness in a certain area. The truth is, however, we don't hate sin as much as we should. Once we allow sin a foothold in one area, it will affect all areas of our lives.

Sin will manifest itself one way or another through anger, bitterness, unkind thoughts, criticism, pride, self-conceit, lack of understanding, impatience, weak prayers, faithlessness in the study of God's Word, lack of fellowship, or a resistance to worship. It's imperative that we discover our weaknesses. Twice Haggai the prophet said, "Consider your ways" (Hag. 1:5, 7). First Kings 8:38 says, "Know every man the plague of his own heart."

2. Fix your heart on God

In Psalm 57:7 David writes, "My heart is fixed, O God, my heart is fixed." His heart was undivided and committed to God. Paul expressed the same thing when he said, "[Oh] that I may know [Christ]" (Phil. 3:10). Psalm 119:6 says, "I shall not be ashamed when I look upon all Thy commandments" (NASB*). If I obey all God's commandments, I will never have reason to be ashamed. Fix your heart on the Lord by learning how to worship Him. That will act as a preservative against a shameful life.

3. Meditate on God's Word

The psalmist said, "Thy word have I hidden in mine heart, that I might not sin against thee" (Ps. 119:11). Don't just read a page from your Bible, close the text, and forget it. That's not meditating on God's Word.

Some people wonder how I get so much from the Bible. When I merely read it, I forget what I read, too. To get to know the Bible I spend hour after hour reading one portion of Scripture until my soul is inextricably woven with what I've read. Once I've done that, I meditate on the thoughts that passage brings to mind night and day. As you meditate on God's Word, it ferrets out of your life the sins it condemns.

4. Pray diligently

First Peter 4:7 tells us to "watch unto prayer." We are to pray diligently. When I'm studying God's Word, it's difficult to separate where my studying ends and my meditating and praying begin. Commune with God when you read, meditate, and pray over His Word.

True prayer will have a strong element of confession. You need to recognize the vileness of sin. When you confess your sin to God, you renew your hatred of it. Don't be concerned only with gross sins—confess any sin in your life. John Owen said, "He who pleads with God for the remission of sin also pleads with his own heart to detest it" (*Sin & Temptation*, p. 47). When you pray about the sin in your life, you remind yourself

New American Standard Bible.

35

that God hates it and that you also should hate it. Prayer becomes a source of strength in times of need (Heb. 4:16). If you are honest enough with God to confess your sin, you will find the strength to kill it. Don't think that just because you kill some sins now you will be free from them forever. But you will see their recurrence decrease over time.

When you come before God in prayer, you open yourself up to Him. He will reveal your heart to you and unmask the sins you normally don't see. Unless you spend that kind of honest time with God, you will never uncover the hidden sins in your life.

5. Have a passion to obey God

You ought to have a consuming passion to obey God. First Peter 1:22 says, "Ye have purified your souls in obeying the truth through the Spirit." When you obey God, you purify your heart. There's nothing mystical about experiencing victory over sin: when you are tempted, you can choose to either sin or obey God. When you obey God, you kill sin and purify your heart.

C. Sustained

Despite knowing the pattern for victory, it's still hard to kill sin. It's especially difficult to eliminate a problem you've had all your life. You'll be tempted to become frustrated when continually dealing with a problem, but fight that by knowing that in time you'll notice more frequent victories and less frequent failures.

How to Confirm Your Salvation

When I first came to Grace Church, I was only twenty-nine and still young in my spiritual development. I went through a time when I wondered if I was really saved. I understood theologically how a person became saved—that wasn't the problem. I had not yet seen evidence in my life of maturity in Christ, and I wasn't consistently defeating sin. While attending college and seminary I was busy learning facts, but I wasn't growing much spiritually. But once I got involved in the ministry at Grace Church, my spiritual growth skyrocketed. Since then, I have never doubted my salvation. It wasn't my theology that confirmed my salvation. Knowing I was getting rid of sin in my life is what confirmed God's presence in me.

When you become more successful at killing sin in your life through God's power, your hatred for it will increase. Consequently, the sins you still struggle with will seem worse than the many you had before you became a Christian. Your battle with sin will continue as long as you live. Don't let anyone tell you he has learned how to stop struggling with sin. No one attains perfection until he dies.

Growing in grace (2 Pet. 3:18), perfecting holiness (2 Cor. 7:1), and renewing the inner man (2 Cor. 4:16) are simply other ways of referring to killing sin. You don't grow by gaining biblical knowledge; you grow by applying it. It pains me to see people who do not apply what they learn about God because they won't experience victory over sin.

Are You Defeating Sin?

Here's what you need to consider:

1. How is your zeal for God?

   Has sin made your heart cold toward God? How much do you desire to worship and commune with Him? The psalmist wrote, "Rivers of waters run down mine eyes, because they keep not thy law" (Ps. 119:136). Do you feel like crying when you or others disobey God? You should be consumed with the desire to obey God and glorify His name.

2. How much do you love God's Word and prayer?

   Your greatest joys should be reading the Bible and praying to the Lord.

3. How much do you love to be with God's people?

   Spending time with fellow Christians should be a higher priority than personal recreation. Don't be like the Jewish people of Malachi's day who grew weary of serving God and said, "Behold, what a weariness is it!" (Mal. 1:13).

4. How sensitive are you to sin?

Can you say with David, "Zeal of thine house hath eaten me up; and the reproaches of those who reproached thee are fallen upon me" (Ps. 69:9)? Do you grieve when there is sin in your or someone else's life?

In Romans 13:14 Paul says, "Put ye on the Lord Jesus Christ, and make not provision for the flesh, to fulfill its lusts."

V. OUR GRATITUDE FOR VICTORY

Romans 8:12 says, "We are debtors, not to the flesh." That implies we are debtors to the Spirit. You and I should be so humbled by what God has done for us that we want to repay Him. Although we will never be able to do that, we can show our gratitude. Jesus bought us with His own precious blood. He paid the supreme price to regenerate us and bring us into His family. Our debt to Him is to live after the Spirit.

Paul wrote Philemon to ask him to take back a wayward slave named Onesimus who had recently become a Christian. He said, "Thou owest unto me even thine own self" (v. 19). If Paul could say that to Philemon, how much more could Christ say that to us!

Luke 17:10 says, "When ye shall have done all those things which are commanded you, say, We are unprofitable servants; we have done that which was our duty to do." All that we are and ever hope to be makes us debtors to Christ. And the longer we have been saved, the greater our debt to Him. The message of Romans 8:12-13 is simple: we are to kill the sin in our lives.

When Julius Caesar was murdered, the people of Rome were enraged and took revenge on his assassins. They burned their homes and possessions. Many of the conspirators were killed. Remind yourself constantly that sin killed the Lord Jesus Christ. May the passion you have against sin be as intense as the passion the Roman people had against those who killed Caesar.

Focusing on the Facts

1. What does Romans 8:12-13 focus on? How is that indicated? Explain (see p. 24).
2. Why wouldn't we be able to kill sin without the Holy Spirit's presence in us (see pp. 24-25)?
3. What are the weapons the Spirit has given us capable of doing (2 Cor. 10:5; see p. 25)?
4. How can we resolve the battle between the flesh and the Spirit (see p. 26)?
5. Why do we not always experience victory over sin (see p. 26)?
6. What does it mean to be filled with the Spirit (see pp. 26-27)?
7. Explain why being filled with the Spirit (Eph. 5:18) and letting the Word of Christ dwell in you (Col. 3:16) are the same thing (see p. 27).
8. What does living a Spirit-filled life require (see pp. 27-28)?
9. Who experiences victory over sin (see p. 28)?
10. Discuss the privileges believers have as a result of what Christ has done (see pp. 28-29).
11. What did Paul mean when he said, "If ye live after the flesh, ye shall die" (Rom. 8:13; see p. 30)?
12. According to Philippians 3:9-14 how did Paul live (see pp. 31-32)?
13. What is the most convincing proof of a believer's salvation (2 Pet. 1:5-10; see p. 32)?
14. What does the word "mortify" in Romans 8:13 indicate regarding sin (see pp. 32-33)?
15. Will you ever ascend to a level in this life where conflict with sin never occurs? Explain (see p. 33).
16. What is the first thing you must do to kill sin (see p. 34)?
17. What does it mean to have your heart fixed on God (see p. 35)?
18. What is the benefit of meditating on Scripture (see p. 35)?
19. What must true prayer include? What does that help you to do (see pp. 35-36)?
20. What are the benefits of prayer (see p. 36)?
21. Although we could never pay the debt we owe for our salvation, what should we do (see p. 38)?

Pondering the Principles

1. Is your life under the control of the Holy Spirit and God's Word? Can you honestly say that your heart, soul, and mind

are saturated with God's truth? Living a Spirit-filled life is the key to having victory over sin. When you meditate on God's Word, it controls your mind, which controls your behavior. Write a list of the sins you need to deal with in your life. Next to each write out Scripture passages referring to that particular sin. Meditate on those passages this week so they will automatically come to mind whenever you need to deal with a specific sin.

2.   Write down all the privileges you enjoy as a result of Christ's death on the cross—privileges that apply now and in the future. What should be your response to God for all those blessings? Don't ever take those great privileges for granted!

3.   Read Philippians 3:13-14. Paul wanted to progress toward perfection. How much effort do you expend toward living a holy life? Read the following verses and specify the command that appears in each one: Romans 12:1-2, 1 Corinthians 6:19-20, Ephesians 5:8-11, Philippians 2:12-15, 2 Timothy 2:19-21, and 1 Peter 2:11-12. Are you living out each command? Do you see in your life the results of obeying them all?

4.   Review the section on the practical ways to kill sin in your life (pp. 12-14). Examine your life carefully to see if you are applying each in a consistent manner. As you read, make a list of the things you need to work on so you can better resist sin. As another means of resisting sin, commit to memory this stanza of Charles Wesley's hymn "Soldiers of Christ, Arise":

> Leave no unguarded place, no weakness of the soul;
> Take ev'ry virtue, ev'ry grace, and fortify the whole.
> From strength to strength go on, wrestle and fight and
>   pray;
> Tread all the pow'rs of darkness down and win the well-
>   fought day.

3

The Spirit Confirms Our Adoption

Outline

Introduction

Review

Lesson
 I. We Are Led by the Spirit (v. 14)
     A. Illumination
     B. Sanctification
        1. Confirmation from the Spirit
        2. Conviction by the Spirit
 II. We Are Freed by the Spirit (v. 15)
     A. Fear of God's Punishment
     B. Freedom in God's Presence
III. We Are Confirmed by the Spirit (v. 16)

Conclusion
 A. Be Fruitful (2 Peter 1)
 B. Be Obedient (1 John 3)

Introduction

Romans 8:14-16 says, "As many as are led by the Spirit of God, they are the sons of God. For ye have not received the spirit of bondage again to fear; but ye have received the Spirit of adoption, whereby we cry, Abba, Father. The Spirit himself beareth witness with our spirit, that we are the children of God." That passage speaks about our relationship with God. The key word is *adoption*: we are "the sons of God" and "the children of God" because we have been adopted.

Adoption speaks of love, mercy, and grace. It is a legal action whereby a person is brought into a family in which he has no blood relations. When a person is adopted, he is given all the privileges that the other members of the family possess.

Second Corinthians 6:17-18 says, "Come out from among them, and be ye separate, saith the Lord, and touch not the unclean thing; and I will receive you, and will be a Father unto you, and ye shall be my sons and daughters, saith the Lord Almighty." The Lord adopts those who separate themselves from evil and come to Him.

God first extended adoption to the Israelites (Rom. 9:4). Then God extended adoption to all the redeemed of Christ's church, predestining "us unto the adoption of sons by Jesus Christ to himself, according to the good pleasure of his will" (Eph. 1:5).

Those who are saved have received the Spirit of adoption and have been made sons of God. Even though we are unworthy, God has made us His children.

Review

We find the theme of Romans 8 in verse 1: "There is . . . no condemnation to them who are in Christ Jesus." Paul began the chapter with that thought and ended with it as well (v. 34). We will not have to be punished for our sins because Christ has already paid the penalty.

The entire chapter demonstrates our no-condemnation status, which is based on the work of the Holy Spirit. It is a discourse on the believer's security. That's why it ends, "What shall separate us from the love of Christ? . . . [Nothing] shall be able to separate us from the love of God, which is in Christ Jesus, our Lord" (vv. 35, 39). The Holy Spirit secures our no-condemnation status by freeing us from sin and death (vv. 2-3), enabling us to fulfill God's law (v. 4), changing our nature (vv. 5-11), and empowering us for victory (vv. 12-13).

Lesson

The Holy Spirit also confirms our adoption, which assures us that we are children of God. He did that by placing us into the family of God through the miracle of regeneration. He trans-

42

ferred us from an alien family into God's family and repeatedly confirms that reality in our hearts.

Today, many think of those who are adopted as second-class offspring—those added to a family because no one else wanted them. But in the first century, people held a very different view of adoption.

In ancient Roman society, if a father didn't deem any of his own sons worthy of inheriting his name and estate, he would adopt a son for that purpose. He would find someone with the character and talents he wanted in a son. The adopted son would then take precedence over all the man's real sons. In ancient Roman culture an adopted son was not a waif picked up off the street. Rather, he was chosen by a father to inherit his estate and bear his name.

When the Bible says we have become the adopted sons of God, it doesn't mean God picked us up off the street just to care for us. It does mean He has chosen us to bear His name and inherit His estate. We don't become children of God through a process of natural birth; we become His children because He sovereignly chose us. That's the essence of the biblical concept of adoption.

The Consequences of Adoption

In Roman society, there were three consequences to being adopted.

1. The adopted person lost all ties to his old family

   An adopted person gained all the rights of the natural children in his new family. That's a beautiful picture of what happens at salvation.

2. The adopted person became an heir of his new father

   The existence of natural-born children did not affect the adopted child's rights. He was a co-heir—and sometimes the sole heir—if that's what the father wanted. The adopted child was considered as real a child as any natural-born children.

3. The adopted person's past was forgotten

   When a person was adopted, all his legal debts were canceled. He was given a new name, as if he had just been born. The same thing happened when you came to

Christt: you were adopted into God's family, all your past debts were canceled, and you became a co-heir of all that the Son possesses.

All those things happened when we were adopted into God's family. We are legally and eternally the sons of God.

Although the word *adoption* is beautiful and rich in meaning, it is insufficient to explain all that happens to us when we become Christians. We are not only adopted, but also regenerated (2 Cor. 5:17). Both adoption and regeneration explain how God brings us to Himself. As adopted people, we are named "sons of God" and given title to an inheritance. Regeneration gives us the nature of sons and makes us fit for our inheritance.

We are under no condemnation because we have been adopted into God's family. All our former debts have been canceled. Since He has made us His children and established our right to be in His presence, no one can condemn us, because there is no higher court than God's court.

Romans 8:15 says we have received "the Spirit of adoption." The Holy Spirit confirms in our hearts the reality of our adoption in three ways.

I. WE ARE LED BY THE SPIRIT (v. 14)

"As many as are led by the Spirit of God, they are the sons of God."

If you can see the Spirit of God leading your life, you can be sure you belong to God because He gives His Spirit only to His children (v. 9). By the Spirit's power you are killing the deeds of the body (v. 13), which also proves you are being led by the Holy Spirit and must therefore be a son of God. Although you won't always obey God as you should, if you sense the Spirit's leading, you are a child of God.

How does the Holy Spirit lead a person? He doesn't lead forcefully; He leads by changing the will. When the Lord redeems people, He doesn't leave them on their own—He promises to lead them.

A. Illumination

The Spirit directs our path by helping us to understand God's Word. Sometimes He may lead us in a specific,

44

practical way but primarily He illuminates the Word of God. As we read, study, and meditate on the Bible, the Spirit opens our hearts and minds to understand it.

1. Genesis 41:38-39—"Pharaoh said unto his servants, Can we find such an one as this is, a man in whom the Spirit of God is? And Pharaoh said unto Joseph, Forasmuch as God hath shown thee all this, there is none so discreet and wise as thou art." When the Egyptians observed Joseph's wisdom, they acknowledged that the Spirit of God was in him. Today we receive God's wisdom through His Word.

2. Ephesians 1:15-19—Paul said, "After I heard of your faith in the Lord Jesus, and love unto all the saints, [I] cease not to give thanks for you, making mention of you in my prayers: that the God of our Lord Jesus Christ, the Father of glory, may give unto you the spirit of wisdom and revelation in the knowledge of him, the eyes of your understanding being enlightened; that ye may know what is the hope of his calling, and what the riches of the glory of his inheritance in the saints, and what is the exceeding greatness of his power toward us who believe."

3. Ephesians 3:16-19—Paul prayed we would "be strengthened with might by [God's] Spirit . . . to know the love of Christ, which passeth knowledge."

4. Colossians 1:9—Paul said, "[We] do not cease to pray for you, and to desire that ye might be filled with the knowledge of his will in all wisdom and spiritual understanding." The Spirit fills us with the knowledge of God's will, and He does that primarily by illuminating the Bible for us. That's why Colossians 3:16 says we are to "let the word of Christ dwell in [us] richly." When we do that, God's Word comes alive to us.

5. 1 Corinthians 2:14—"The natural man receiveth not the things of the Spirit of God; for they are foolishness unto him, neither can he know them, because they are spiritually discerned." The non-Christian cannot understand Scripture on his own—it has to be spiritually defined for him. But those under the teaching ministry of the Spirit are able to discern all things (vv. 13-15). Verse 16 says that such a person has "the mind of Christ."

6. Luke 24:45—Christ opened the disciples's "understanding, that they might understand the scriptures." Although Christ explained the Scriptures, the Holy Spirit did the illuminating work.

Do You Question Your Salvation?

The primary way the Spirit leads us is by illuminating the Bible. If you question your salvation, ask yourself these questions: *Am I understanding God's Word? Is the Spirit teaching me its truths? Am I coming to accurate conclusions about what I learn from the Bible? Is my heart convicted when I read it? Does God's Word give me joy when I read the joyful passages? Does it make me sorrowful when I read the sad passages? Is the Bible a living book to me?* If you can say yes to those questions, the Spirit has been illuminating God's Word for you. Anyone can read the Bible, but not everyone can have it illuminated in his heart.

B. Sanctification

Once the Holy Spirit has shown us what God's Word says, He assists us in applying what we've learned. He not only illumines our minds but also stirs our hearts and wills. The Spirit lives within us, speaks to our hearts and minds, convicts us, and produces His fruit in us: love, joy, peace, patience, gentleness, goodness, faith, meekness, and self-control (Gal. 5:22-23). The Spirit leads by prompting our hearts to obey God.

The psalmist said, "Make me to go in the path of thy commandments; for therein do I delight" (Ps. 119:35). He also said, "Order my steps in thy word, and let not any iniquity have dominion over me" (v. 133). The Spirit of God illuminates the mind and activates the will.

1. Confirmation from the Spirit

Notice that Romans 8:14 is in the present tense: "As many as are led by the Spirit of God, they are the sons of God." When you are not studying God's Word or walking in obedience, you won't receive confirmation of your salvation from the Spirit. When you do not submit to His leading, you will doubt your salvation. That's why the New Testament is filled with exhortations to be obedient and growing in God's Word. If we always responded to the Spirit's illuminating and sanctifying work in our lives, we wouldn't need exhortation. Although we are led by the Spirit, we don't follow Him like we should.

Contrary to popular belief, being led by the Spirit is not a life filled with ecstatic moments. The Spirit's leading is not a sporadic, momentary thing. It's a continuing reality in the life of every believer.

2. Conviction by the Spirit

Without the Spirit's help, you would have many problems. He restrains sin in you—it is through Him that you kill the deeds of the body (Rom. 8:13). The Holy Spirit battles with you against sin. He doesn't leave you to fight sin alone, even if you fail to resist it. He convicts you and leads your mind, heart, and will to go in the right direction. When you are tempted to sin, you hear His voice. If you fall, you hear His voice again: "Why did you do that?" He painfully convicts you so you will never want to commit that sin again.

In Galatians 5:16 Paul says, "Walk in the Spirit, and ye shall not fulfill the lust of the flesh." If you follow the path the Spirit leads you on, you won't sin. In verses 17-21 Paul explains, "The flesh lusteth against the Spirit, and the Spirit against the flesh. . . . If ye be led by the Spirit, ye are not under the law. Now the works of the flesh are manifest, which are these: adultery, fornication, uncleanness, lasciviousness, idolatry, sorcery, hatred, strife, jealousy, wrath, factions, seditions, heresies, envyings, murders, drunkenness, revelings, and the like." Instead, you will produce the fruit of the Spirit (vv. 22-23). Paul concluded, "If we live in the Spirit, let us also walk in the Spirit" (v. 25).

Are You Grieving the Holy Spirit?

It is possible for you to grieve and quench the Holy Spirit's work in your life (Eph. 4:30; 1 Thess. 5:19). It is also possible to insult the Spirit of grace (Heb. 10:29). If you do that you will forfeit whatever assurance the Holy Spirit produces in your heart. One aspect of the peace He produces in you is a contented heart that is right with God. If you don't follow the Spirit's leading in your life, you will lose that peace.

II. WE ARE FREED BY THE SPIRIT (v. 15)

"Ye have not received the spirit of bondage again to fear; but ye have received the Spirit of adoption, whereby we cry, Abba, Father."

The Spirit affirms we belong to God, which prompts us to cry, "Abba, Father." That's the second way the Spirit affirms our adoption.

A. Fear of God's Punishment

Before you became a Christian, you were in bondage to sin. Hebrews 2:15 says, "[Christ came to] deliver them who, through fear of death, were all their lifetime subject to bondage." Men live under the guilt of sin and fear of judgment. The unredeemed feel a sense of bondage—they don't have the relief that salvation provides. Unsaved people may try to forget or evade their fear, or use man-made religions to cover it up, but by doing those very things they affirm their fear. In the conscience of man, "the law [of God] worketh wrath" (Rom. 4:15).

You didn't become a Christian to receive a spirit of bondage. The Spirit of God wants to confirm your no-condemnation status; He doesn't want you to have an unhealthy fear of punishment, damnation, or losing your salvation. He came into your life to confirm that you belong to God. In fact God's love is "shed abroad in our hearts by the Holy Spirit" (Rom. 5:5). Second Timothy 1:7 says, "God hath not given us the spirit of fear, but of power, and of love, and of a sound mind." John said, "Perfect love casteth out fear" (1 John 4:18). Since God revealed perfect love to us through Christ, there's no need for us to fear.

The Holy Spirit is "the Spirit of adoption" (Rom. 8:15), but you will sense His confirming work only when you walk in the Spirit. As soon as you stop following His lead, you will forfeit your sense of assurance.

B. Freedom in God's Presence

The Holy Spirit frees our minds and hearts from any fear of punishment, moving us to cry out, "Abba, Father." The Greek word translated "cry" in Romans 8:15 (*krazō*) means "to cry loudly with deep emotion." "Abba" is an Aramaic term that means "Papa" or "Daddy." Its use is appropriate for only one person—your father. It's a personal term reflecting trust, dependence, intimacy, tenderness, and love. Our Lord used it when He spoke to the Father in the Garden of Gethsemane (Mark 14:36).

The Holy Spirit's presence in our hearts allows us to come before God. We were once sinners living in fear; now we are sons in the care of our beloved heavenly Father. We were once strangers; now we are intimate friends. We can go into the presence of a holy God and say, "Papa!"

The Holy Spirit gives us a deep sense of intimacy with God. Do you ever share with God the deepest things in your heart? Do you say to Him, "I need to talk to You about this problem"? The Spirit prompts our hearts to come into God's presence. There's no need for us to fear God's wrath because the Holy Spirit gives us the sense of freedom to come to God in intimate fellowship.

III. WE ARE CONFIRMED BY THE SPIRIT (v. 16)

"The Spirit himself beareth witness with our spirit, that we are the children of God."

In Roman society, an adoption had to be confirmed. According to Roman law, there had to be seven witnesses to an adoption (William Barclay, *The Letter to the Romans* [Philadelphia: Westminster, 1957], p. 111). That's how important adoption was. The reason for so many witnesses was to prevent the natural children in a family from denying the adopted child his share of the inheritance when the father died. When the father died, the witnesses were to come forward and confirm the adopted person's status. Likewise, the Holy Spirit bears testimony that you are a child of God.

Someone might say to you, "I don't think you have any right to inherit God's throne. I've seen the way you act; I doubt you're a Christian." Or perhaps you sinned and are doubting your salvation. But remember: the Holy Spirit witnessed your adoption and bears witness with your spirit that you are a child of God. That's why Paul said no one can condemn you (Rom. 8:34), including Satan, the great accuser (Rev. 12:10).

Many people claim they're children of God when it isn't true. They don't have the confirmation of the Spirit. If they claim that long enough, they may eventually convince themselves that they are children of God, but they still won't

49

have the Spirit's confirmation. Only those who truly belong to Him will receive that confirmation.

Conclusion

A. Be Fruitful (2 Peter 1)

Peter tells us God has given us "exceedingly great and precious promises, that . . . ye might be partakers of the divine nature, having escaped the corruption that is in the world through lust. . . . Beside this, giving all diligence, add to your faith virtue; and to virtue, knowledge; and to knowledge, self-control; and to self-control, patience; and to patience, godliness; and to godliness, brotherly kindness; and to brotherly kindness, love" (vv. 4-7). All that happens when you walk in the Spirit. If you live in the freedom He gives you and hear His voice as He leads you, you will be fruitful (v. 8). But there is a warning for those who don't: "He that lacketh these things is blind and cannot see afar off, and hath forgotten that he was purged from his old sins" (v. 9).

Assurance of salvation comes from the fruit produced in your life when you walk in the Spirit. He wants to lead you, have you cry, "Abba, Father," and assure you that you are redeemed. But you will experience that only when you let Him illuminate God's Word to you and submit to His prompting to obey the Lord. If you don't, you will become blind and forget that you were saved. Verses 10-11 conclude, "Give diligence to make your calling and election sure [to yourself]; for if ye do these things, ye shall never fall. For so an entrance shall be ministered unto you abundantly into the everlasting kingdom of our Lord and Savior, Jesus Christ."

You cannot enjoy your no-condemnation status unless you are responding to the Spirit's leading and prompting. If you're not walking in obedience to God's will, you will not sense the Spirit's leading. If you are not following His promptings to come to God, you won't feel as if you have access to God—you will feel like you can't pray. Nor will you sense the affirming testimony of the Holy Spirit when you question your salvation. Only those who walk in the Spirit will have that affirmation.

B. Be Obedient (1 John 3)

John said, "My little children, let us not love in word, neither in tongue, but in deed and in truth. And by this we know that we are of the truth, and shall assure our hearts before him" (vv. 18-19). How can you know you are a Christian and that you belong to Christ? By being sure that you don't just love in word, but in deed and truth. Then John said, "If our heart condemn us, God is greater than our heart, and knoweth all things. Beloved, if our heart condemn us not, then have we confidence toward God. And whatever we ask, we receive of him, because we keep his commandments, and do those things that are pleasing in his sight. And this is his commandment, that we should believe on the name of his Son, Jesus Christ, and love one another, as he gave us commandment. And he that keepeth his commandments dwelleth in him, and he in him. And by this we know that he abideth in us, by the Spirit whom he hath given us" (vv. 20-24).

When you walk in obedience, your heart won't condemn you. It is the Holy Spirit who gives you that assurance (v. 24). He assures you of your no-condemnation status by affirming that you have been adopted as God's child. The Spirit's ministry is constant—it's when we walk away from His leading that we lose the confidence He gives us.

A nineteenth-century Cornish evangelist named Billy Bray was so excited about what God was doing in his life that he just couldn't help praising the Lord. As he walked along the street, he said one foot seemed to say, "Glory!" and the other, "A-men!" When you think about what God has done for us, you too can say, "Glory," and, "Amen!"

Focusing on the Facts

1. Explain what adoption is (see pp. 41-42).
2. Whom does the Lord adopt (2 Cor. 6:17-18; see p. 42)?
3. What role did adoption have in ancient Roman society? What does it mean to become the adopted sons of God (see p. 43)?
4. If you can sense the Spirit of God leading your life, what can you be sure of (Rom. 8:14; see p. 44)?
5. What is the first way the Spirit leads us? Explain (see pp. 44-45).

6. What was Paul's point in 1 Corinthians 2:14 (see p. 45)?
7. After the Holy Spirit has shown us what God's Word says, what does He do (see p. 46)?
8. Romans 8:14 is in the present tense. Why is that significant (see p. 46)?
9. Why is the New Testament filled with exhortations (see p. 46)?
10. Paraphrase the following verse: "Walk in the Spirit, and ye shall not fulfill the lust of the flesh" (Gal. 5:16). If we walk in the Spirit, what will we produce (vv. 22-23; see p. 47)?
11. What happens when a Christian grieves the Holy Spirit (see p. 47)?
12. What is the second way the Holy Spirit affirms our adoption by God? Explain (see p. 48).
13. What do unsaved people live in fear of? Why shouldn't Christians have that fear (see p. 48)?
14. What is significant about being able to say, "Abba, Father" (Rom. 8:15; see pp. 48-49)?
15. Why did Roman law require witnesses when an adoption took place? How does the Holy Spirit's testimony of our adoption comfort us (see p. 49)?
16. What are we admonished to do in 2 Peter 1:5-7? What will be the result if we do those things (v. 8)? What will happen if we don't (v. 9; see p. 50)?
17. According to 1 John 3:18-19 how can you know if you are a Christian (see p. 51)?

Pondering the Principles

1. There were three consequences to being adopted into a family in Roman society (see pp. 43-44). Those same things happened when you were adopted into the family of God. Read Romans 6:3-8, 16-18, and Ephesians 4:21-24. What former life did you leave when you became saved? What family were you adopted into (2 Cor. 6:18; Gal. 3:26)? What does 1 Peter 1:4 say about your inheritance? According to Psalm 103:12, Isaiah 43:25, and Jeremiah 31:34, what does God do with past sins once they are forgiven? Read Colossians 1:9-13. God has made you fit for His Son's kingdom. Thank Him for your adoption into His family.

2. The Holy Spirit's presence in our hearts allows us to come before God without fear of punishment. We now can have deep fellowship with the Father. Think of several ways that a father cares for his child (e.g., providing guidance and showing love). In the same way God wants to show father-

ly care for you. Do you give Him the opportunity to do that? Describe your relationship with the Father. Do you share with Him the deep things of your mind and heart? Do you ask Him for wisdom and comfort in the midst of trials? What can you do to make your relationship with the Father all that it should be? Commit yourself to developing a deeper and more meaningful relationship with your heavenly Father.

3. Are there times when you question your salvation? Read 2 Peter 1:5-10 carefully. Are all the qualities mentioned in verses 5-7 present in your life? According to verse 8, what will happen if you have those qualities? Usually when a person doubts his salvation, it's because he cannot see fruit in his life. Your level of commitment to God will affect how secure you feel in your relationship with Him. Whenever you begin to question your salvation, examine your life to make sure you are being obedient and letting "the word of Christ dwell in you richly" (Col. 3:16).

4
The Gain of Glory

Outline

Introduction

Review

Lesson
I. The Incomparable Gain of Glory (vv. 17-18)
    A. The Heirs of Glory
    B. The Source of Glory
    C. The Extent of Glory
        1. It is equal
        2. It is endowed
        3. It is eternal
    D. The Proof of Glory
        1. The fact of suffering
        2. The result of suffering
        3. The consolation in suffering
    E. The Comparison of Glory

Conclusion

Introduction

Every Christian lives in the hope of glory to come. Our hope is best summed up in 1 John 3:2: "When [Christ] shall appear, we shall be like him; for we shall see him as he is." David said, "I will behold thy face in righteousness; I shall be satisfied, when I awake, with thy likeness" (Ps. 17:15). Our great hope is to be in heaven in God's presence and be like Christ. The theme of Romans 8:17-30 is our hope of such glory.

Review

In Romans 8 the Holy Spirit confirms our no-condemnation status before God. He does that by freeing us from sin, enabling us to fulfill God's law, changing our nature, empowering us for victory, and confirming our adoption.

Lesson

The climax of it all is that the Holy Spirit affirms we will not be condemned by guaranteeing our heavenly glory. He does so by giving us confidence in our hearts and confirmation in our minds. Romans 8:30 sums up verses 17-29: "Whom [God] did predestinate, them he also called; and whom he called, them he also justified; and whom he justified, them he also glorified." Whoever is justified (made right with God through Jesus Christ) will be glorified. That's what Jesus meant when He said, "This is the Father's will who hath sent me, that of all that he hath given me I should lose nothing" (John 6:39).

There is no salvation without glorification. One of the tenses of salvation is future: a person's salvation is not real unless it embraces the future. Some claim a person can become saved but lose his salvation, thus forfeiting glorification. That's not possible because inherent in the truth of salvation is a guarantee of future glory. Romans 8:29 says, "Whom he did foreknow, he also did predestinate to be conformed to the image of his Son." Before you were saved, God planned to save you and conform you to Christ's image. Thus glorification completes the reality of salvation.

The goal of our salvation is eternal glory. The Holy Spirit confirms that truth by placing hope in our hearts—we are saved in hope (Rom. 8:24).

Restoring Our Glory

Man was created in the image of God (Gen. 1:26). Therefore he had a glorious beginning. He was honored and respected. He was without sin and radiated the essence of God's Person. But when man sinned, he lost his glory, dignity, and honor. He lost the beauty that was his in creation. That's why Romans 3:23 says man has "come short of the glory of God."

I believe we all know instinctively that we are devoid of glory (cf. Rom. 1:18-21). That's why so many seek self-esteem, expending tremendous effort to find self-satisfaction and gain respect. As comedian Rodney Dangerfield says, "I don't get no respect!" Innate in man is a longing to get back the glory he senses is missing. In his quest he fills himself with ambition, pride, and jealousy. He tries to rise above others but still cannot regain his former glory. Post-Fall man cannot know pre-Fall glory. But in Christ that glory is restored.

One day we who are Christians will be transformed: we will fully reflect God's glory and be found in His likeness (Ps. 17:15). We will be like Christ. We won't return to Eden but will go beyond Eden, for perfection is better than innocence. We will know a radiant glory that far exceeds the glory Adam and Eve had before they sinned.

The great British preacher Martyn Lloyd-Jones rightly observed, "Salvation cannot stop at any point short of this entire perfection" (*Romans*, vol. 6 [Grand Rapids: Zondervan, 1980], p. 7). Man, in Christ, is reserved for glory (Rom. 8:29-30). Romans 8 concludes that nothing can separate us from the love of Christ (vv. 35-39). No one will be able condemn us (v. 34) or "lay any thing to the charge of God's elect" (v. 33). Whomever God justifies, He glorifies (v. 30). There's no such thing as salvation without glorification.

Second Corinthians 3:18 says, "We all, with unveiled face [nothing hindering our vision] beholding as in a mirror the glory of the Lord, are changed into the same image from glory to glory, even as by the Spirit of the Lord." As we gaze at the glory of the Lord, we are changed into the same image from one level of glory to the next. While we are on earth, the Holy Spirit takes us through different levels of glory. He lifts us up by restoring our dignity. Little by little, as we look at the glory of the Lord, the Spirit restores the honor we lost in the Fall. That is a constant work until finally, when we see Christ, we reflect His full glory. Salvation is the path to glory. Once you begin that path you must come to its end, because the essence of salvation is being conformed to the image of Christ.

I. THE INCOMPARABLE GAIN OF GLORY (vv. 17-18)

"If [we are] children, then [we are] heirs—heirs of God, and joint heirs with Christ—if so be that we suffer with him, that we may be also glorified together. For I reckon that the sufferings of this present time are not worthy to be compared with the glory which shall be revealed in us."

Paul introduced the theme of glorification by linking it with the prior passage dealing with our adoption. Romans 8:14-16 affirms that we are children of God. Verse 17 builds on that: "If children, then heirs—heirs of God, and joint heirs with Christ." "If" (Gk., *ei*) is not an expression of doubt—it is a first-class condition in the Greek text, something that affirms the reality of a statement. The best translation for *ei* is "since." Since we are children of God, we are also heirs. Galatians 3:26 specifies exactly who the children of God are: "Ye are all the sons of God by faith in Christ Jesus." If you put your faith in Christ, you are a son of God and an heir. It is impossible to be a son of God and not be an heir. You will receive what has been promised to the heirs of God and joint heirs with Christ.

A. The Heirs of Glory

Hebrews 1:14 describes angels as "ministering spirits, sent forth to minister for them who shall be heirs of salvation." Christians are "heirs of salvation." James 2:5 says, "Hearken, my beloved brethren, Hath not God chosen the poor of this world to be rich in faith and heirs of the kingdom which he hath promised to them that love him?" Colossians 1:12 says that the Father has made Christians "fit to be partakers of the inheritance of the saints in light."

When you were saved, you were made an heir. God is faithful; He never disinherits anyone. Philippians 1:6 says to be "confident of this very thing, that he who hath begun a good work in you will perform it until the day of Jesus Christ." There is an assurance that if you have been saved, you will receive glory. If you sense the leading of the Spirit and His affirmation that you belong to God, you can be confident that you are a child of God and an heir.

Can a Christian Lose His Inheritance?

When Paul wrote Romans 8 to the church at Rome, he had in mind the Roman custom of adoption. When a child was adopted into a Roman family, he was not considered inferior to any other child of that family. In fact, sometimes the father would consider the adopted child to be superior to the other children. In Jewish culture, the firstborn child received the largest inheritance in the family—a double portion of everything. However, the Roman custom was to give all the children in a family an equal portion of the inheritance—even the adopted children. When Paul said we are all heirs, he was saying we will all receive an equal inheritance. According to Roman law, what a person inherited was considered more secure than anything he had purchased. Paul used Roman customs regarding inheritance to illustrate the security of our no-condemnation status. God will not disinherit one who is His own (cf. John 1:12).

Galatians 3:29 says, "If ye be Christ's, then are ye Abraham's seed, and heirs according to the promise." If you belong to Christ and manifest the same faith that characterized Abraham, then you are an heir. Galatians 4:7 says, "Thou art no more a servant, but a son; and if a son, then an heir of God through Christ."

B. The Source of Glory

Romans 8:17 says that we who are the children of God are also "heirs of God." God is the source of our inheritance—we receive it directly from Him. Colossians 3:24 says, "Of the Lord ye shall receive the reward of the inheritance." God gives us the inheritance, and He gives it at His own sovereign discretion. One day the King shall say, "Come, ye blessed of my Father, inherit the kingdom prepared for you from the foundation of the world" (Matt. 25:34). God prepared the kingdom as an inheritance for us before the creation of the world! Because He never changes (Mal. 3:6; cf. Ps. 90:2) we can be sure He will keep His promise. Some of us are heirs of people who don't have much to give. But as heirs of God, we will possess more than we can ever imagine!

The psalmist wrote, "Whom have I in heaven but thee? And there is none upon earth that I desire beside thee" (Ps. 73:25). Jeremiah wrote, "The Lord is my portion" (Lam. 3:24). That's the mature perspective on our inheritance: in the midst of all that God possesses, our most treasured possession is God Himself. Revelation 21:3 says that in the New Jerusalem, "The tabernacle of God [will be] with men, and he will dwell with them, and they shall be his people, and God himself shall be with them, and be their God." The best part of the inheritance is God Himself.

59

C. The Extent of Glory

Romans 8:17 says we are joint heirs "with Christ." We will receive an inheritance as extensive as the one Christ will receive. That's a staggering thought because everything will be brought into subjection to Christ.

Paul said, "Blessed be the God and Father of our Lord Jesus Christ, who hath blessed us with *all* spiritual blessings in heavenly places in Christ" (Eph. 1:3; emphasis added). God will "gather together in one all things in Christ, both which are in heaven, and which are on earth, even in him" (v. 10). Ultimately everything belongs to Christ, and that is the extent of our inheritance.

1. It is equal

Hebrews 1:1-2 says, "God, who at sundry times and in diverse manners spoke in time past unto the fathers by the prophets, hath in these last days spoken unto us by his Son, whom he hath appointed heir of all things." Since Christ is heir of all things and we are joint heirs with Him, we too are heirs of all things. That is strictly an act of grace because Christ has a right to His inheritance; we do not. We receive it only through Him.

Romans 8:17 says we will be glorified together with Christ. Paul said, "Ye know the grace of our Lord Jesus Christ, that, though he was rich, yet for your sakes he became poor, that ye through his poverty might be rich" (2 Cor. 8:9). Jesus prayed, "Father, glorify thou me with thine own self with the glory which I had with thee before the world was" (John 17:5). We will receive that same glory. We won't be equal to Christ in terms of deity, but we will be equal to Him in the sense that we will inherit all that He possesses. You won't find any "No Trespassing" or "Forbidden" signs in heaven! Jesus also prayed, "The glory which thou gavest me I have given them [His disciples]" (John 17:22). That includes us (v. 20). We ought to think about our future inheritance more often. It's easy to become bogged down with earthly things. Instead we should dwell on heavenly things (2 Cor. 4:18; Col. 3:2).

2. It is endowed

The greatness of our inheritance is beyond human comprehension. We received it by grace, not by good works (Titus 3:5-7). We didn't do anything to deserve it. Far from starting off as children of God, we were of our father, the devil (John 8:44). We had to be adopted to become heirs, and God adopted us by His sovereign will (Rom. 8:30). Titus 3:7 says, "Being justified by His grace, we should be made heirs according to the hope of eternal life." Hebrews 9:15 says Christ died so that "they who are called might receive the promise of eternal inheritance."

3. It is eternal

First Peter 1:4-5 says we have been promised "an inheritance incorruptible, and undefiled, and that fadeth not away, reserved in heaven for you, who are kept by the power of God." Everything on earth grows old, becomes defiled, or fades away. But the believer's inheritance is incorruptible and eternal. We who are saved don't need to work at staying saved; we are kept by God's power. We will receive the inheritance promised us before the world began (Eph. 1:3-4). That is truly cause for rejoicing (Rom. 5:2)!

D. The Proof of Glory

Paul said, "If so be that we suffer with him . . . we may be also glorified together" (Rom. 8:17). Where is the proof that we will be glorified? It comes through suffering. We endure persecution, mockery, scorn, and ridicule because of our union with Christ. You can recognize those who are children of God because the world doesn't like them.

The persecution Christians receive goes to many extremes. Some Christians receive light affliction while others are martyred. But we have all been ostracized or looked down upon for our faith in Jesus Christ. Those who suffer for Christ are the heirs of God (Rom. 8:17). You will be glorified with the Lord if you are suffering for Him.

1. The fact of suffering

Romans 8:17 is better translated, "Since we are children, we are heirs—heirs of God, and joint heirs with Christ—inasmuch as we suffer with him." Paul assumed that Christians would suffer. As he said in 2 Timothy 3:12, "All that will live godly in Christ Jesus shall suffer persecution." There's no way around some form of persecution—it's part of being a Christian. It's proof that we belong to Christ. Suffering is a necessary element in our lives.

In 2 Timothy 2:11-12 Paul says, "It is a faithful saying: For if we be dead with [Christ], we shall also live with him; if we suffer, we shall also reign with him." The hostile, God-hating, Christ-rejecting world doesn't like believers because they live in contrast to their sinfulness. Therefore we shouldn't be surprised when we endure persecution. Jesus said, "[Since] the world hate you, ye know that it hated me before it hated you" (John 15:18). Don't run from persecution and compromise the gospel. Too much of that goes on today in Christianity. Many are unwilling to pay the price for their faith.

2. The result of suffering

The more you suffer, the more you grow. First Peter 5:10 says, "The God of all grace, who hath called us unto his eternal glory by Christ Jesus, after ye have suffered awhile, [will] make you perfect." The more you grow, the more you are able to glorify the Lord. Why do we have to suffer? Because the more we suffer here, the greater will be our capacity to glorify God in eternity.

a) 2 Corinthians 4:8-18

Paul said, "We are troubled on every side, yet not distressed; we are perplexed, but not in despair; persecuted, but not forsaken; cast down, but not destroyed; always bearing about in the body the dying of the Lord Jesus" (vv. 8-10). Paul and his companions lived on the edge of death. He continued, "We who live are always delivered unto death for Jesus' sake. . . . Death worketh in us, but life in you" (vv. 11-12). There was a cost in spreading the gospel. Paul and his companions suffered that others might benefit. Nevertheless, "though our outward man perish, yet the inward man is renewed day by day" (v. 16). Those who suffer for Christ receive an inward dose of divine strength.

Paul continued, "Our light affliction, which is but for a moment, worketh for us a far more exceeding and eternal weight of glory" (v. 17). The more you suffer now, the greater will be your capacity for glory in the life to come. As believers we will be rewarded (1 Cor. 3:12-15; 2 Cor. 5:10). I believe those rewards are capacities to radiate the glory of God, serve Him, and take in the fullness of our inheritance—all based in part on how much we've suffered for Christ.

The more you suffer here, the more you will learn about God, be infused with His strength, and be fit to bear an "eternal weight of glory." That puts suffering in a whole new light. Since we will be spending eternity with God, we want to glorify Him as much as possible, so that gives us incentive not to fear suffering. Someone once said to me, "I would like to join your church, but I'm afraid of what my mother would say." Scripture teaches that whatever ostracism we experience now is only "light affliction" that works in us "a far more exceeding and eternal weight of glory" (2 Cor. 4:17). Paul ended 2 Corinthians 4 with these wise words: "We look not at the things which are seen, but at the things which are not seen; for the things which are seen are temporal, but the things which are not seen are eternal" (v. 18).

b) 1 Peter 1:6-8

Peter said, "In this [our inheritance] ye greatly rejoice, though now for a season, if need be, ye are in heaviness through manifold trials, that the trial of your faith, being much more precious than of gold that perisheth, though it be tried with fire, might be found unto praise and honor and glory at the appearing of Jesus Christ, whom, having not seen, ye love." Our suffering will pay off in glory when Christ returns. Our eternal capacity to glorify God depends on our willingness to suffer now for the sake of Christ. Those most capable of glorifying God in eternity will be those who suffered the most for Christ.

3. The consolation in suffering

Second Corinthians 1:5 says, "As the sufferings of Christ abound in us, so our consolation also aboundeth by Christ." The degree to which you suffer is the degree to which Christ brings peace to your heart. There's no need to fear anything.

Some people are afraid to suffer for Christ because they think they won't be able to handle it. People wonder how I can stand the criticism I receive for upholding biblical truth. I do receive negative mail, but for every negative letter I receive, I enjoy the consolation of God's Spirit. I wouldn't trade that for anything. I'd rather say what needs to be said and get persecuted than not stand firm for Christ. When I take a stand for Christ, the light affliction I receive confirms that I will have a greater capacity to glorify the Lord. That's why Paul said he longed for "the fellowship of [Christ's] sufferings" (Phil. 3:10). To the Galatians he said, "I bear in my body the marks of the Lord Jesus" (6:17). To the Colossians he said, "[I] fill up that which is behind of the afflictions of Christ in my flesh for his body's sake, which is the church" (1:24). He considered it a privilege to bear the blows of the One who suffered so for Him.

Suffering for Christ in this sin-cursed, Christ-hating world is normal for Christians. We should be willing to endure persecution because through it, we not only receive the consolation of the Spirit but also acquire a greater capacity to glorify God in eternity. Romans 8:17 ends by declaring that we will be glorified together with Christ. He suffered, so we will suffer. He is glorified, so we will be glorified with Him. There's no health-and-wealth or peace-and-prosperity doctrine in Christianity. Christians who avoid conflict with the world limit their potential for reflecting the glory of God for eternity.

E. The Comparison of Glory

Paul was willing to suffer because he was convinced "that the sufferings of this present time are not worthy to be compared with the glory which shall be revealed in us" (Rom. 8:18). The Greek word translated "sufferings" (*pathēma*) refers to the suffering of persecuted Christians in 1 Peter 5:9 and the sufferings of Christ in Hebrews 2:10. Our current sufferings for the cause of Christ are not worthy to be compared to what we will receive in the age to come. Any suffering in this world is trivial when compared to future glory. That's a comforting thought in the darkest hour of a trial.

When unbelievers suffer, they have no hope. I've seen non-Christian mothers who lost a baby look into the casket, lift the baby out, and cling desperately to him, fearing they will never see him again. They have no hope because they don't know Christ (1 Thess. 4:13). Unbelievers have no just anticipation for the future. But those of us who are believers know everything will be right in Christ's kingdom. We know that there will be justice, riches, and no pain. We live in light of that hope. Because we know the glory to be revealed in us is far beyond anything that pain could give us, we consider the suffering we endure not worth worrying about. Instead we dwell on the "eternal weight of glory" (2 Cor. 4:17).

Conclusion

The Holy Spirit tells us we are sons of God. He confirms that by giving us the freedom to cry, "Abba, Father," and assuring our spirits that we belong to God (Rom. 8:15-16). Since we are children of God, we are His heirs. And since we are heirs, we will inherit glory so magnificent that it makes everything in this life of pain fade into utter insignificance. In light of that may "the very God of peace sanctify you wholly; and I pray God your whole spirit and soul and body be preserved blameless unto the coming of our Lord Jesus Christ. Faithful is he that calleth you, who also will do it" (1 Thess. 5:23-24).

Focusing on the Facts

1. What does every Christian live in the hope of? How is that hope best summed up (see p. 55)?
2. How does the Spirit affirm our future glory (see p. 56)?
3. Can a person become saved and never become glorified? Explain (see p. 56).
4. Why do so many people in the world today seek self-esteem (see pp. 56-57)?
5. Explain 2 Corinthians 3:18 (see p. 57).
6. Who are the heirs of glory? Explain (see p. 58).

7. Does God ever disinherit anyone? What assurance do we have of that (see p. 58)?
8. From whom will we receive our inheritance? Support your answer with Scripture (see p. 59).
9. What is significant about being joint heirs with Christ (see p. 60)?
10. How did we receive our inheritance (Titus 3:5-7)? Explain (see p. 61).
11. How does 1 Peter 1:4-5 describe our inheritance (see p. 61)?
12. What is the proof that we will be glorified (Rom. 8:17; see pp. 61-62)?
13. What Scriptures support the fact that Christians will suffer persecution (see pp. 61-62)?
14. Explain the comparison Paul made in 2 Corinthians 4:17. What is its significance (see p. 63)?
15. According to 2 Corinthians 1:5, what will we receive along with the sufferings we endure for Christ (see p. 64)?
16. Why should a Christian be willing to suffer (Rom. 8:18; see pp. 64-65)?

Pondering the Principles

1. Some people teach that just because a person is saved, that doesn't necessarily guarantee him future glorification. But the Holy Spirit repeatedly assures us in the Bible that whoever is saved will also be glorified. Read Ephesians 1:15-18; Colossians 1:3-5, 27; and Titus 1:1-2; 3:4-7. What relationship do you see between salvation and glorification in those passages? What effect should the knowledge that you will someday receive glory in heaven have on your life? What effect should that knowledge have on your relationship with God?

2. Second Corinthians 3:18 declares that the Holy Spirit is changing us from one level of glory to another. As we behold Christ, the Spirit makes us more and more like Christ. In what way is it possible for you to limit the Spirit's work in your life? How can you prevent that? What characteristics in your life have been changed since you became a Christian? What characteristics still need to be worked on? Are you willing to let them be changed? Thank God for the Holy Spirit's work in your life and don't hold back from Him the things that need to be worked on.

3. In Romans 8:18 Paul says, "I reckon that the sufferings of this present time are not worthy to be compared with the

glory which shall be revealed in us." How much do you suffer for Christ's sake? Have you ever been overwhelmed in your suffering? What do you focus on when you suffer for Christ, and what kind of attitude do you have? It's easy to feel like you're are drowning when enduring persecution. What should you focus on in times like that? Write Romans 8:18 on a small card and put it where you will see it frequently during this week. Let Paul's words become ingrained in your heart so that when you suffer for Christ, you will be comforted from dwelling on the "glory which shall be revealed in us."

5
Creation's Groans for Glory

Outline

Introduction

Review
I. The Incomparable Gain of Glory (vv. 17-18)

Lesson
II. The Inexpressible Groans for Glory (vv. 19-27)
   A. The Groan of Creation (vv. 19-22)
      1. The longing of creation (v. 19)
         a) Its poetic personification
         b) Its patient anticipation
      2. The subjection of creation (v. 20)
         a) Its futility
         b) Its victimization
         c) Its hope
      3. The restoration of creation (v. 21)
         a) The liberation of creation
         b) The liberation of Christians
      4. The pain of creation (v. 22)

Conclusion

Introduction

Paul's great letter to the Romans is basically a gospel presentation. Paul said his purpose was to articulate "the gospel of God" (1:1, 15). After stating his reason for presenting the gospel and his commitment to it (vv. 13-17), Paul used the remainder of his letter to present the substance, benefits, and results of the gospel.

First Paul presented mankind's need for salvation (1:18–3:20). Next he discussed the saving work of Christ—the great doctrine of justification by faith (3:21–5:21). Then he related all the benefits and results of salvation (chapters 6-8) to the doctrine of sanctifications, which explains what it means to have been made holy in Christ Jesus.

What are the results of salvation? Because we have been justified in Christ, we are considered dead to sin. We also have union with Christ and have become servants to righteousness (Rom. 6). We are freed from the penalty of God's law. We are a new creation that wars against sin. Now our delight is in the law of God (Rom. 7). Yet perhaps the most monumental benefit is that "there is, therefore, now no condemnation to them who are in Christ Jesus" (Rom. 8:1). The concept that a person could become permanently justified before God was foreign to Jewish and pagan tradition. So Paul uses Romans 8 to explain that truth.

Review

In our study of Romans 8 we have noted that the Holy Spirit confirms our no-condemnation status by freeing us from sin, enabling us to fulfill the law, changing our nature, empowering us for victory, and confirming our adoption. The final element is that the Holy Spirit guarantees our glory. When you were saved, God planted His Holy Spirit in you, and that was your guarantee of glory.

Reinforcing the Guarantee

The Holy Spirit assures that it is impossible for you to lose your salvation.

1. Ephesians 1:13-14—In Christ, "in whom ye also trusted, after ye heard the word of truth, the gospel of your salvation; in whom also after ye believed, ye were sealed with that Holy Spirit of promise" (v. 13). When you were saved, you were forever sealed for God, and nothing can break that seal. Verse 14 continues, "[The Holy Spirit] is the earnest [ancient Gk., *arrhabōn*, "down payment" or "first installment"; modern Gk., "engagement ring"] of our inheritance until the redemption of the purchased possession." When you were saved, you were purchased

by God. You haven't entered into your full inheritance yet, but the Spirit is the guarantee that you will one day.

2. Philippians 1:6—"[Be] ye confident of this very thing, that he who hath begun a good work in you will perform it until the day of Jesus Christ." When God begins a work, He finishes it. The Holy Spirit is the agent of His work: we will enter into the fullness of the inheritance guaranteed to us by the indwelling presence of the Spirit.

3. Colossians 3:3-4—"Ye are dead, and your life is hidden with Christ in God. When Christ, who is our life, shall appear, then shall ye also appear with him in glory."

4. 1 Thessalonians 5:23-24—Paul said, "The very God of peace sanctify you wholly; and I pray God your whole spirit and soul and body be preserved blameless unto the coming of our Lord Jesus Christ. Faithful is he that calleth you, who also will do it."

Those passages verify that we will enter into the inheritance promised to us—"the redemption of the purchased possession" (Eph. 1:14). One day we will receive the fullness of our salvation, and God's promise of that is kept in us by the power of the Holy Spirit.

The Holy Spirit's guarantee of our glory is summed up in Romans 8:30: "Whom [God] did predestinate, them he also called; and whom he called, them he also justified; and whom he justified, them he also glorified." All believers will be glorified. There is no doubt. There is no such thing as salvation without glorification. No one can lose his or her salvation. It is the work of God that He began in eternity past, brought to reality in the present, and will fulfill in the future. God's promise of glorification is central to salvation, and it *must* be fulfilled (Rom. 8:30). If someone appears to have been saved but abandons the faith, that's evidence the person never was saved (1 John 2:19).

I. THE INCOMPARABLE GAIN OF GLORY (vv. 17-18; see pp. 57-65)

"If children, then heirs—heirs of God, and joint heirs with Christ—if so be that we suffer with him, that we may be also glorified together. For I reckon that the sufferings of this present time are not worthy to be compared with the glory which shall be revealed in us."

Lesson

II. THE INEXPRESSIBLE GROANS FOR GLORY (vv. 19-27)

Three things groan in these verses: creation (v. 22), believers (v. 23), and the Holy Spirit (v. 26). These groans are laments over living in this world of sin and pain. The Greek word translated "groan" means "to lament" or "moan." The groans in this passage are groans for glory.

A. The Groan of Creation (vv. 19-22)

"The earnest expectation of the creation waiteth for the manifestation of the sons of God. For the creation was made subject to vanity, not willingly but by reason of him who hath subjected the same in hope. Because the creation itself also shall be delivered from the bondage of corruption into the glorious liberty of the children of God. For we know that the whole creation groaneth and travaileth in pain together until now."

Paul took poetic license in personifying creation as groaning in sorrow over its present plight.

Anticipating the New Heavens and Earth

The Lord declared, "Behold, I create new heavens and a new earth, and the former shall not be remembered, nor come into mind" (Isa. 65:17). The Jewish people anticipated the day when all oppression, anxiety, and persecution would end and their dream of a new world would become a reality.

Some of the unbiblical Jewish writings of Paul's day expanded on that promise. For example, in the Apocalypse of Baruch we read, "The vine shall yield its fruit ten thousand fold, and on each vine there shall be a thousand branches; and each branch shall produce a thousand clusters; and each cluster produce a thousand grapes; and each grape a cor of wine. And those who have hungered shall rejoice; moreover, also, they shall behold marvels every day. For winds shall go forth from before me to bring every morning the fragrance of aromatic fruits, and at the close of the day clouds distilling the dews of health" (29:5). The people were looking forward to a utopia. In the Sibylline Oracles we find this: "Earth, and all the trees, and the innumerable flocks of sheep shall give their true fruit to mankind, of wine

72

and of sweet honey and of white milk and of corn, which to men is the most excellent gift of all" (3:620-33).

Elsewhere in the Sibylline Oracles we read, "Earth, the universal mother, shall give to mortals her best fruit in countless store of corn, wine and oil. Yea, from heaven shall come a sweet draught of luscious honey. The trees shall yield their proper fruits, and rich flocks, and kine, and lambs of sheep and kids of goats. He will cause sweet fountains of white milk to burst forth. And the cities shall be full of good things, and the fields rich; neither shall there be any sword throughout the land or battle-din; nor shall the earth be convulsed any more, nor shall there be any more drought throughout the land, no famine, or hail to work havoc on the crops" (3:744-56). Those are not inspired accounts, but they do reflect some of what Scripture says we have to look forward to when God recreates the world.

1. The longing of creation (v. 19)

"The earnest expectation of the creation waiteth for the manifestation of the sons of God."

a) Its poetic personification

What part of creation is longing for that new age? It couldn't be the angels, because they aren't subject to corruption—they aren't longing for another state. It couldn't be demons, because they will never share in any glorious liberation. They have been sentenced to eternal bondage. It couldn't be believers, since verse 23 distinguishes their groans from the groaning of creation. And it couldn't be unbelievers, because they have no hope.

Now that we have eliminated rational creation, all that's left is animate and inanimate irrational creation: plants, animals, mountains, hills, stars, seas, rivers, lakes, sky, earth, and flowers. Romans 8:19-22 personifies them in poetic fashion. We see that elsewhere in Scripture. Isaiah 35:1 says, "The wilderness and the solitary place shall be glad." Isaiah 55:12 says, "The mountains and the hills shall break forth before you into singing, and all the trees of the field shall clap their hands." Those verses personify the joy creation will have when it enters the glory of its future state.

73

b) Its patient anticipation

Creation has an "earnest expectation." That translates a very vivid word in the Greek text. It refers to someone standing on the tips of his toes, sticking his neck way out to see something in the distance. In a sense, nature is on its tiptoes peering into the future. The Greek word translated "waiteth" means "to wait patiently but expectantly." It refers to anticipation and readiness. Nature is on its tiptoes, filled with expectation, ready for the dawning of a new age.

What is nature looking for? "The manifestation of the sons of God." The Greek word translated "manifestation" means "unveiling." All creation is waiting for the unveiling "of the sons of God"—when believers enter into their perfect state.

First John 3:2 says, "Beloved, now are we the children of God, and it doth not yet appear what we shall be, but we know that, when [Christ] shall appear, we shall be like him; for we shall see him as he is." When we walk on a street or go into a market, the people around us don't know that we have the eternal glory of God dwelling in us. Some might notice our smiles and something of a glow about us, but for the most part unbelievers don't know who we are. That's because we are still veiled by our humanness. But all creation waits for our unveiling.

One day we will be glorified. Romans 8:18 says that it will be a glory without comparison. Colossians 3:4 says, "When Christ, who is our life, shall appear, then shall ye also appear with him in glory." One day we will be free from sin and the flesh, basking in Christ's presence in blazing purity. Creation anticipates the time when the saints will shine as stars forever (Dan. 12:3; cf. Matt 13:43).

2. The subjection of creation (v. 20)

"The creation was made subject to vanity, not willingly but by reason of him who hath subjected the same in hope."

a) Its futility

The Greek word translated "vanity" (*mataiotēs*) means "futility" or "aimlessness." It speaks of the inability to fulfill a purpose or a desired result. Nature can't be what it was designed to be—it can't fulfill its reason for existing, which is to reflect God's perfect glory. Nature is therefore frustrated.

Genesis 1:31 says God "saw every thing that he had made, and, behold, it was very good." There were no weeds (Gen. 3:17-18). There was no sin or curse. The Garden of Eden flourished. Adam didn't have to work to maintain the Garden; he just picked food whenever he wanted. The earth was perfect. But when man sinned, nature was subjected to futility. It can no longer reflect God's perfection.

In the Greek text the phrase "the creation was made" contains a verb in the aorist tense: what happened to creation happened in a moment of time in the past. By some momentary act, the earth became subject to futility. Nature became a victim of decay, corruption, and frustration. That's why there's smog, pollution, and deterioration on the earth. The Sierra Club and other environmentalists won't be able to stop that. They make sincere attempts to do so, but the earth will continue to fall short of its full potential because it is subjected to futility. Occasionally we get a glimpse of creation in its splendor when observing a beautiful flower or a gorgeous, clear day in the wilderness. That gives us an idea of what the earth was like before it was cursed.

b) Its victimization

The verb in the phrase "the creation was made" is passive, which means that creation didn't make itself subject to futility—something else did. Creation was victimized. It was unwillingly subjected to futility.

When Adam and Eve sinned God said, "Because thou hast harkened unto the voice of thy wife, and hast eaten of the tree, of which I commanded thee, saying, Thou shalt not eat of it: cursed is the ground for thy sake; in sorrow shalt thou eat of it all the days of thy life; thorns also and thistles shall it bring forth to thee; and thou shalt eat the herb of the field; in the sweat of thy face shalt thou eat bread, till thou return unto the ground; for out of it wast thou taken: for dust thou art, and unto dust shalt thou return" (Gen. 3:17-19).

God's curse brought decay, disaster, pollution, and degeneration. It was necessary for Him to do that so man would not be able to find perfection anywhere—even in outer space. God wants us to understand the tremendous effect of sin: it does not pollute just the one who sins; its ramifications are endless. One man's sin polluted an entire universe.

Nature's destiny is inseparably linked to that of man. Because man sinned, creation fell. When man is restored to the glorious state that God has planned for His children, creation will likewise be restored. There will be a new heaven and earth (Rev. 21:1)—an uncursed, eternally glorious domain that perfectly reflects God's glory.

c) Its hope

Nature is looking for the glorious manifestation of the children of God because that's when it will be freed from the bondage of corruption.

The Deterioration of the World

An incredible connection exists between man's sin and the decay of the universe. In the physical sciences the law of entropy states that the order of a system tends to become disorganized and random. There is disintegration everywhere because of the curse, and that is emphasized in Romans 8. The theory of evolution is not true because it is opposite the truth: the universe is not in an upward trend but in a downward trend. It's moving from absolute perfection to total disaster. Everything will end in a devastating holocaust brought about by God. You need not be afraid of total nuclear war because the Bible doesn't say the Soviet Union or any other nation will blow up the whole world. The earth will still be around at Christ's second coming. He will recreate it Himself. The world will come to an end only when the Lord causes it to do so.

76

Creation is looking for that great time "in hope" (Rom. 8:20). In Revelation 21:1-4 the apostle John says, "I saw a new heaven and a new earth; for the first heaven and the first earth were passed away, and there was no more sea. And I, John, saw the holy city, new Jerusalem, coming down from God out of heaven, prepared as a bride adorned for her husband. And I heard a great voice out of heaven saying, Behold, the tabernacle of God is with men, and he will dwell with them, and they shall be his people, and God himself shall be with them, and be their God. And God shall wipe away all tears from their eyes; and there shall be no more death, neither sorrow, nor crying, neither shall there be any more pain; for the former things are passed away." That's what creation is so eagerly waiting to see. And it will happen at the unveiling of the glorious children of God. But until then creation groans because it, along with mankind, remains under God's curse.

3. The restoration of creation (v. 21)

"The creation itself also shall be delivered from the bondage of corruption into the glorious liberty of the children of God."

Creation is looking for the time when it will be restored. The Greek verb translated "delivered" is passive—creation will be renewed by God, not by itself.

a) The liberation of creation

Second Peter 3 describes what will happen: "The day of the Lord will come as a thief in the night" (v. 10). A thief doesn't make much noise; he moves quietly when people least expect him. That's how the Day of the Lord will come. The rest of verse 10 continues, "The heavens shall pass away with a great noise, and the elements shall melt with fervent heat; the earth also, and the works that are in it, shall be burned up." That's what happens in an atomic explosion, though I doubt that atom bombs will destroy the earth. I think the destruction will be atomic in that God will disintegrate the atoms of the universe and set forth a chain reaction beyond anything we can imagine. Everything will be burned up. Verse 11 says that "all these things shall be dissolved [Gk., *luō*, "set loose"]." Atoms that are bound together will be split. Verse 12 says that in "the coming of the day of God . . . the heavens, being on fire, shall be dissolved, and the elements shall melt with fervent heat." After all that, there will be "new heavens and a new earth, in which dwelleth righteousness" (v. 13).

All creation is on its tiptoes, looking off into the horizon, awaiting a cosmic regeneration. Everything will be renewed. Christ said to His disciples, "Ye who have followed me, in the regeneration, when the Son of man shall sit on the throne of his glory, ye also shall sit upon twelve thrones, judging the twelve tribes of Israel" (Matt. 19:28). Acts 3:21 refers to "the times of restitution of all things." Everything will be the way God wants it to be. There will be no sin, evil, pain, sorrow, death, or tears. Everything will be glorious. Creation longs for that. It will get an initial taste of that glory in the millennial kingdom (Rev. 20:4), and the full taste in the glorious new heavens and earth.

Romans 8:21 says, "Creation itself also shall be delivered from the bondage of corruption." The stain of sin in the world holds creation in bondage. There's no way to stop the law of entropy. The disintegration of our universe is consistent—it cannot be reversed. We see decay even in our social institutions. Everything man touches turns to ashes.

Creation is bound in corruption, but it will be delivered. However, only God can reverse the curse—nature can't release itself from bondage.

b) The liberation of Christians

When nature is freed, it will be delivered "into the glorious liberty of the children of God." Paul said, "For this corruptible must put on incorruption, and this mortal must put on immortality" (1 Cor. 15:53). We will all have new bodies (vv. 51-54). Jesus in His glorified body was able to walk through walls and eat, so what we have to look forward to will be amazing in one sense and familiar in another.

78

Those of us who are Christians have great hope for the future. We know where the world is going. God, the great environmentalist, will restore the whole earth Himself. Since "our citizenship is in heaven" (Phil. 3:20), creation isn't alone in its groaning. We too are on our tiptoes looking forward to when we are delivered into glorious liberty. We eagerly anticipate the time when we will be liberated from the bondage of corruption. As Paul said, "We look for the Savior, . . . who shall change our lowly body, that it may be fashioned like his glorious body" (vv. 20-21).

4. The pain of creation (v. 22)

"We know that the whole creation groaneth and travaileth in pain together until now."

"Until now" means "up to the present." "Groaneth" literally means "to groan together." All the elements of creation are groaning in harmony about their cursed state. How great is the evil of sin! The next time you try to justify a sin, remember that if you had committed the first sin, you would have polluted the universe. Bible commentator Richard Haldane wrote, "As the leprosy not only defiled the man who was infected with it, but also the house he inhabited, in the same way, sin, which is the spiritual leprosy of man, has not only defiled our bodies and our souls, but, by the just judgment of God, has infected all creation" (*An Exposition of the Epistle to the Romans* [Fla.: MacDonald, 1958], p. 372).

Verse 22 says that creation "travaileth in pain," a reference to the pain of childbirth. The pain creation endures is not futile—it leads to something good. The pain of childbirth is one pain a woman can look forward to because it brings a child into the world. That pain was a part of the curse in Genesis 3:16, yet it brings forth something good. In a similar way the groaning of the earth precedes the new age.

Conclusion

Martyn Lloyd-Jones had the wonderful ability to grasp insights from Scripture. Musing over Paul's vivid personification of creation in Romans 8 he observed, "Nature every year, as it were, makes an effort to renew itself, to produce something permanent; it has come out of the death and the darkness of all that is so true of the Winter. In the Spring it seems to be trying to produce a perfect creation, to be going through some kind of birth-pangs year by year. But unfortunately it does not succeed, for Spring leads only to Summer, whereas Summer leads to Autumn, and Autumn to Winter. Poor old Nature tries every year to defeat the 'vanity', the principle of death and decay and disintegration that is in it. But it cannot do so. It fails every time. It still goes on trying, as if it feels things should be different and better; but it never succeeds. So it goes on 'groaning and travailing in pain together until now'. It has been doing so for a very long time . . . but Nature still repeats the effort annually" (*Romans*, vol. 6 [Grand Rapids: Zondervan, 1980], pp. 59-60).

Focusing on the Facts

1. According to Ephesians 1:13-14 what happened when you became a believer (see pp. 70-71)?
2. According to Philippians 1:6 what can we be confident of (see p. 71)?
3. Why are creation, believers, and the Holy Spirit groaning (see p. 72)?
4. What did the Jewish people of Paul's day look forward to? Explain (see pp. 72-73).
5. Paul said that creation is longing for a new age (Rom. 8:19). What part of creation was he referring to? How do you know (see p. 73)?
6. What does "earnest expectation" (Rom. 8:19) refer to (see p. 74)?
7. What is creation waiting for (see p. 74)?
8. What does it mean that "the creation was made subject to vanity" (Rom. 8:20)? Discuss the significance of the aorist tense and passive voice (see p. 75)?
9. Who subjected creation to its futility? Why (see pp. 75-76)?
10. What is nature's destiny inseparably linked to (see p. 76)?
11. What does Revelation 21:1-4 say the new age will be like (see p. 77)?
12. According to 2 Peter 3:10-12 what will happen on "the day of the Lord" (see pp. 77-78)?
13. What will creation be delivered from one day (Rom. 8:21)? Who will bring about that deliverance (see p. 78)?
14. What will happen when we are glorified (see pp. 78-79)?

15. Romans 8:22 says creation "travaileth in pain together." What does that phrase refer to? How is that similar to the pain of childbirth (see p. 79)?

Pondering the Principles

1. In Romans 8:19 Paul says, "The anxious longing of the creation waits eagerly for the revealing of the sons of God" (NASB). Read Matthew 13:43, 1 Corinthians 15:51-54, Philippians 3:21, and 1 John 3:2. Using those verses, write down everything you can learn about what will happen when we are glorified. How does our present, unglorified state differ from what you have listed?

2. Write down some of the things you appreciate about animate and inanimate creation (for example, the song of a bird or the beauty of wild flowers). What are some things about nature that manifest God's wisdom (such as the way God designed penguins to tolerate freezing temperatures)? Add those things to your list. Praise God for the magnificence of His creation!

3. Can you think of ways that nature has been affected by man's sin? (For some clues, see Genesis 3:18, Isaiah 24:6, Jeremiah 12:4, and the contrast provided by Isaiah 11:6-9.) Look up the following verses: Psalm 5:4-6; Proverbs 6:16-19; 15:8-9, 26; and Habakkuk 1:13. According to those verses, how does God view sin? Just as sin is ugly to God's eyes, so the impact of man's sin is a blight on nature. Think of several ways that man has had a negative impact on his environment. What would be involved in trying to reverse the damage man has done? Can man completely reverse his negative influence on nature? One day the earth as we know it will be destroyed (2 Pet. 3:10-12), and there will be "new heavens and a new earth, in which dwelleth righteousness" (v. 13). Thank God for the promise of a cosmic regeneration. Thank Him for allowing you to be a part of His perfect, eternal kingdom.

6
Believers' Groans for Glory

Outline

Review
I. The Incomparable Gain of Glory (vv. 17-18)
II. The Inexpressible Groans for Glory (vv. 19-27)
A. The Groan of Creation (vv. 19-22)

Lesson
B. The Groan of Believers (vv. 23-25)
  1. The believer's adoption (v. 23)
    a) The salvation of our bodies
    b) The description of our redeemed bodies
  2. The believer's hope (vv. 24-25)
    a) It is inseparable from salvation (v. 24a)
    b) It is an unseen reality (vv. 24b-25)

Review

Ephesians 1:14 says the Holy Spirit "is the earnest [down payment] of our inheritance until the redemption of the purchased possession, unto the praise of his glory." When you became a Christian, God gave you His Holy Spirit to guarantee that you will make it to glory. He promised you would be glorified, and it is the ministry of the Holy Spirit to carry out that promise. The Spirit guarantees our making it from salvation present to salvation future. He is the down payment on "the purchased possession" of God (Eph. 1:14). Our bodily redemption will not take place until we are glorified. God has put us on layaway and will reclaim us fully in eternity.

I. THE INCOMPARABLE GAIN OF GLORY (vv. 17-18; see pp. 57-65)

II. THE INEXPRESSIBLE GROANS FOR GLORY (vv. 19-27)

In Romans 8:17-30 we find the Greek verb *stenazō* and its noun form *stenagmos*. The verb form means "to sigh" or "groan," and the noun form refers to the groanings or sighings of a person trapped in undesirable or inescapable circumstances. It's used in Acts 7:34, where God says, "I have seen the affliction of my people who are in Egypt, and I have heard their groaning, and am come down to deliver them." He then told Moses He would free the Israelites from their oppression (Ex. 3:7-8). Jesus Himself groaned or sighed when He saw a deaf man suffering as the result of sin (Mark 7:34). Another example of groaning appears in Hebrews 13:17: "Obey them that have the rule over you, and submit yourselves; for they watch for your souls, as they that must give account, that they may do it with joy, and not with grief [groaning]."

There are three groans in Romans 8:19-27: the groan of creation, the groan of believers, and the groan of the Holy Spirit.

A. The Groan of Creation (vv. 19-22; see pp. 72-79)

"The earnest expectation of the creation waiteth for the manifestation of the sons of God. For the creation was made subject to vanity, not willingly but by reason of him who hath subjected the same in hope. Because the creation itself also shall be delivered from the bondage of corruption into the glorious liberty of the children of God. For we know that the whole creation groaneth and travaileth in pain together until now."

Restoring the Universe

The Bible clearly teaches there will be a cosmic regeneration—God will recreate the entire universe. Revelation 21:1 speaks of "a new heaven and a new earth." There are three facets in the restoration of the universe:

1. The destruction of the cursed earth

   The present earth will eventually be destroyed. That won't happen instantaneously; it will take place in phases.

Revelation describes a sequence of events that will occur when the earth begins to fall apart: the sun will be blackened, the moon will become like blood, and stars will fall (6:12-13; cf. Joel 2:10; 3:15). The waters of the earth will be cursed—both salt water (Rev. 8:8-9) and fresh water (Rev. 8:10-11). There will be death everywhere. From the midpoint of the seven-year tribulation period to the end, there will be a sequence of devastating destructions upon the earth. God will systematically destroy the present universe and the people who are set against Him.

2. The establishment of the millennial kingdom

In this age marvelous things will happen: the lion will lie down with the lamb (Isa. 11:6; 65:25), and the desert will blossom like a rose (Isa. 35:1). But that's only the first phase of the restoration—just a taste of what is to come.

3. The establishment of the eternal kingdom

At the end of the millennial kingdom, God will create "a new heaven and a new earth" (Rev. 21:1). That will usher us into the eternal state, where "there shall be no more curse" (Rev. 22:3).

All creation longs for the curse to be removed. That will happen when the Tribulation and the Millennium are over.

Some prophetic passages of the Bible, when describing future glory, describe events that will occur during the Millennium. Others speak of what will occur in the eternal kingdom, when the cosmic regeneration is complete. In Romans 8 Paul is simply saying that creation is groaning for deliverance because it has been polluted by the power of sin. It wasn't his purpose to go into the details of the deliverance itself.

Lesson

B. The Groan of Believers (vv. 23-25)

We who are saved join creation in lamenting the curse of sin. David groaned because his iniquities were like a burden too heavy for him to bear (Ps. 38:4). He said to God, "Lord, all my desire is before thee, and my groaning is not hidden from thee" (v. 9). That's a common lament for Old and New Testament saints. Paul said, "Oh, wretched man that I am! Who shall deliver me from the body of this death?" (Rom. 7:24). We can identify with that—we get tired of our sinfulness.

Paul also said, "We that are in this tabernacle do groan, being burdened; not that we would be unclothed, but clothed upon, that mortality might be swallowed up of life" (2 Cor. 5:4). Wouldn't you like to be rid of the debilitating sinfulness in your flesh? John 11 tells us that Jesus was full of agony when He came to the tomb of Lazarus. He was shaking and sobbing because He saw the terrible consequences of sin. Believers are in the midst of undesirable circumstances. God, by His marvelous grace, gives us joy and blessings, yet we still groan for a better state.

1. The believer's adoption (v. 23)

"Not only they [creation], but ourselves also, who have the first fruits of the Spirit [the guarantee of our glory], even we ourselves groan within ourselves, waiting for the adoption, that is, the redemption of our body."

When you came to Christ in saving faith, your soul was redeemed. The old inner man is gone—you have a new inner man and are a new creation (Col. 3:9-10; 2 Cor. 5:17). A definitive eternal work was accomplished in you. But you still have to deal with your humanness.

We are "waiting for the adoption." Technically we have been adopted, but we haven't entered into the full manifestation of it as yet. Although we already are "the children of God" (Rom. 8:16), our identity as such is not readily apparent to the world. The apostle John said, "Behold, what manner of love the Father hath bestowed upon us, that we should be called the children of God; therefore, the world knoweth us not, because it knew him not. Beloved, now are we the children of God, and it doth not yet appear what we shall be, but we know that, when he shall appear, we shall be like him; for we shall see him as he is" (1 John 3:1-2).

We groan within ourselves because although we know we have been adopted, we must await the redemption of our bodies, which is when we shall be like Christ. Only then will our adoption be complete. We are called the children of God, but we have yet to match our redeemed souls with redeemed bodies. That's why Romans 13:11 says, "Now is our salvation nearer than when we believed." That's a reference to the future aspect of salvation. If you were saved yesterday, that means today you are one day closer to the full redemption of your body.

a) The salvation of our bodies

> Since we were redeemed, we have become new creations in Christ: "Old things are passed away; behold, all things are become new" (2 Cor. 5:17). We have become partakers of the divine nature (2 Pet. 1:4) and are fit for eternal glory. We have been made suitable for heaven. But for now we are in bondage. We have to contend with the lusts, desires, and thoughts of our bodies. The new creation in us is still housed in an earthly body. We are corruptible, mortal, and prone to disease and death. We are human. We are awaiting the salvation of our bodies. Someone might wonder if Christ's atonement provides healing. It does, but not until our bodies are redeemed.

(1) Romans 6

> Paul said, "[Since] we have been planted together in the likeness of [Christ's] death, we shall be also in the likeness of his resurrection" (v. 5). When we were redeemed, we were planted with other believers into Christ's holy likeness. We have His nature. We are a holy seed living in an unholy shell.
>
> Paul continued, "Knowing this, that our old man is crucified with [Christ], that the body of sin might be destroyed" (v. 6). When you were saved, the old man in you was crucified. The "old man" is who you were before salvation. Your unregenerate nature is gone. You don't possess an old and new nature simultaneously. You are a new creation. Sin was able to flourish

87

in the old man. Now that the old man is dead, "we should not serve sin" (v. 6).

But although the old man is dead, sin is still in us. Verse 12 says, "Let not sin, therefore, reign in your mortal body." Before you became saved, you were rotten on the inside and outside. But when you became a Christian, God planted a new nature within you—a holy, incorruptible, eternal creation—but it is encased in the shell of "your mortal body." That includes not only your physical body, but also your lusts, desires, motives, and thoughts.

Verse 13 gives an additional perspective: "Neither yield ye your members as instruments of unrighteousness." "Members" refers to bodily parts. In the purest sense, we can say that sin is in your flesh, not in your soul. Sin is not a part of your new nature.

Verses 17-18 says, "God be thanked, that whereas ye were the servants of sin, ye have obeyed from the heart that form of doctrine which was delivered you. Being, then, made free from sin, ye became the servants of righteousness." Your new nature is free from sin. You have been transformed, but your humanness is still a problem. That's why we look forward to getting redeemed bodies.

(2) Romans 7

In Romans 7 Paul makes personal application from the preceding chapter: "We know that the law is spiritual; but I am carnal, sold under sin. For that which I do I understand not; for what I would, that do I not; but what I hate, that do I" (vv. 14-15). He still battled with sin even as a believer. In verses 16-17 he says, "If, then, I do that which I would not, I consent unto the law that it is good. Now, then, it is no more I that do it, but sin that dwelleth in me" (vv. 16-17). Paul's new nature wasn't giving him problems; it was the sin that dwelled in his humanness. He continued, "I know that in me (that is, in my flesh) dwelleth no good thing. . . . Now if I do that I would not, it is no more I that do it, but sin that dwelleth in me. I find then a law, that, when I would do good, evil is present with me. For I delight in the law of God after the inward man; but I see another law in my members, warring against the law of my mind, and bringing me into captivity to the law of sin which is in my members" (vv. 18, 20-23). Paul concluded, "So, then, with the mind I myself serve the law of God; but with the flesh, the law of sin" (v. 25).

The inner part of us is redeemed and fit for heaven. All God has to do in the future is redeem our bodies. When Paul said, "We ourselves groan within ourselves, waiting for the adoption" (Rom. 8:23), he was referring not to the redemption of our souls, but to our bodies. He said the same thing a different way in Philippians 3:20-21: "Our citizenship is in heaven, from which also we look for the Savior, the Lord Jesus Christ, who shall change our lowly body, that it may be fashioned like his glorious body." That will be "the manifestation of the sons of God" (Rom. 8:19). Inside we are already children of God. The world can't see that because "it doth not yet appear what we shall be, but we know that, when he shall appear, we shall be like him" (1 John 3:2). Then it will be obvious to the whole universe that we are the children of God.

b) The description of our redeemed bodies

What will our new bodies be like? The best description is in 1 Corinthians 15. Our new bodies won't be like the ones we have now. Paul said, "How are the dead raised up? And with what body do they come? Thou fool, that which thou sowest is not made alive, except it die; and that which thou sowest, thou sowest not that body that shall be, but a bare grain, it may chance of wheat, or of some other grain. But God giveth it a body as it hath pleased him, and to every seed its own body" (vv. 35-38). According to Paul, asking what our bodies will be like is silly. If someone puts forty different seeds in your hand, how will you know what each one will look like when it grows? If you aren't a farmer or some other specialist, you wouldn't know a weed seed from any other seed.

89

The seeds in your hand could produce anything from a small weed to a giant tree. We can't predict what our glorified bodies will be like by looking at our present bodies.

Then Paul said, "All flesh is not the same flesh, but there is one kind of flesh of men, another flesh of beasts, another of fish, and another of birds" (v. 39). Different kinds of flesh come from different combinations of amino acids, which will only reproduce themselves. For example, if you eat chicken all your life, you won't grow feathers because no matter what you eat, the amino acids will be converted into what you are made of. Paul was saying that since God has created so many different types of flesh, we cannot speculate on what our new bodies will be like.

Paul continued, "There are also celestial bodies, and bodies terrestrial. . . . There is one glory of the sun, and another glory of the moon, and another glory of the stars; for one star differeth from another star in glory. So also is the resurrection of the dead. It is sown in corruption; it is raised in incorruption. It is sown in dishonor; it is raised in glory. It is sown in weakness; it is raised in power. It is sown a natural body; it is raised a spiritual body" (vv. 40-44).

What did Christ look like after His resurrection? He still had the nail marks and scars from the crucifixion (John 20:20). He still looked like Himself, except that people couldn't recognize Him unless He allowed them (Luke 24:13-16, 30-31; John 20:14-16). He could eat (Luke 24:30), and instantly show up wherever He wanted (John 20:19). In Acts 1:9 He flew up to heaven—perhaps in an instant. The possibilities of what your new body will be like are endless. You'll just have to wait to find out!

Paul ended 1 Corinthians 15 with these thoughts: "We shall all be changed . . . and the dead shall be raised incorruptible. . . . For this corruptible must put on incorruption, and this mortal must put on immortality. . . . Then shall be brought to pass the saying that is written, Death is swallowed up in victory" (vv. 51-54).

90

A Taste of Glory

Why should we be eager for the redemption of our bodies? Because we have within us "the first fruits of the Spirit" (Rom. 8:23). Since the Holy Spirit lives and works in us, displays God's power through us, and shows us God's grace and goodness, He gives us a taste of glory. When I see the Holy Spirit give me victory over sin, I get a taste of what it will be like when I have complete victory over sin in eternity. When the Holy Spirit allows me to praise God, I sense what it will be like to praise Him perfectly. When I see the Spirit help me serve God in a way that brings forth blessing, I get a taste of what it will be like to serve Him without the bondage of mortality. Each taste makes me long for what I could do were I not encumbered by my humanness.

The fruit of the Spirit is love, joy, peace, patience, gentleness, goodness, faith, meekness, and self-control (Gal. 5:22-23). A little taste is all we need to make us want more. Everything we experience of the wonder and power of God's Spirit is only a forctaste of glory.

2. The believer's hope (vv. 24-25)

   a) It is inseparable from salvation (v. 24a)

   "We are saved by hope."

   Hope is an essential element of our salvation. The Greek word translated "saved" is in the aorist passive and implies that our salvation was planned in the past, bestowed in the present, and characterized by hope for the future. Hope is inseparable from salvation because salvation is certain: Jesus said He wouldn't lose any that the Father had given Him (John 17:12). Everyone who comes to Christ is secure in Him. We were saved not only to experience the immediate redemption of our souls but also to have hope in the future salvation of our bodies.

   Hebrews 6:17-19 affirms the believer's security: "God, willing more abundantly to show unto the heirs of promise the immutability of his counsel, confirmed it by an oath, that by two immutable things, in which it was impossible for God to lie, we might have a strong consolation, who have fled for refuge to lay hold upon the hope set before us, which hope we have as an anchor of the soul."

First Thessalonians 5:8 refers to the believer's helmet as "the hope of salvation." I'm saddened for Christians who don't feel secure about their salvation. The reason many believe a person can lose his or her salvation is the result of an inadequate understanding of salvation. Today the gospel has been cheapened, the standard for salvation has been lowered, and many people who are not really saved profess Christ. When those people stop professing Christ, they will appear to have lost their salvation. But if we uphold the standard of the gospel—if we preach the same gospel Jesus did—people won't think they're saved when they aren't.

What about a Christian who doesn't believe in the security of the believer? A true Christian can think he is going to lose his salvation, but he won't. What he will lose is the joy of being a Christian. If you are truly saved, you are saved in hope. A person's salvation is not real unless it has a future fulfillment.

b) It is an unseen reality (vv. 24b-25)

"Hope that is seen is not hope; for what a man seeth, why doth he yet hope for? But if we hope for that which we see not, then do we with patience wait for it."

Although our hope is not something we can see, it is still a reality. If you hold something in your hand, you don't say, "I'm hoping for this," because you already have it. You don't hope for what you see. We have been saved, but our bodies aren't yet redeemed. Therefore, we hope for "the redemption of our body" (Rom. 8:23).

We have confidence that "he who hath begun a good work in [us] will perform it until the day of Jesus Christ" (Phil. 1:6). That isn't wishful thinking—that is confident assurance! First Peter 1:13 says, "Gird up the loins of your mind [think clearly], be sober, and hope to the end for the grace that is to be brought unto you at the revelation of Jesus Christ." Live in constant anticipation of what will happen to you when Christ is revealed in glory.

When I sin, I long for the redemption of my body. I don't let sin depress me; instead, I anticipate the greater reality awaiting me. And the reality of my hope affects the way I live because I have confidence in my future salvation. I'm secured by the Holy Spirit.

Paul commended the Thessalonians, saying, "[We remember] without ceasing your work of faith, and labor of love, and patience of hope in our Lord Jesus Christ" (1 Thess. 1:3). You can labor in love and service to Christ only by having the hope that one day you will be glorified with Him. The Christian is not a fatalist or a pessimist. We were saved in hope and wait patiently for our glorification. There is a better day coming. Creation sighs for that day, and so do we.

Focusing on the Facts

1. Explain the meaning of the Greek word *stenazō* (see p. 84).
2. What will happen in the first phase of the restoration of the universe (see pp. 84-85)?
3. What will happen when the millennial and eternal kingdoms are established (see p. 85)?
4. What does every child of God groan about (see pp. 85-86)?
5. What happened when you came to Jesus Christ in saving faith (see p. 86)?
6. Why does Paul say we are "waiting for the adoption" (Rom. 8:23) when he said previously we were already "the children of God" (Rom. 8:16; see p. 86)?
7. What does Paul mean when he said, "Now is our salvation nearer than when we believed" (Rom. 13:11; see p. 87)?
8. What important biblical concept does Paul mention in Romans 6:5 (see p. 87)?
9. Why do Christians still sin, even though the old man in us is crucified with Christ? What constitutes our "mortal body" (Rom. 6:12; see pp. 87-88)?
10. Why did Paul struggle with sin (Rom. 7:14-25; see pp. 88-89)?
11. What does Paul say about what our new bodies will look like (1 Cor. 15:35-38; see pp. 89-90)?

12. Why should we be eager for the redemption of our bodies (Rom. 8:23; see p. 91)?
13. What does hope have to do with our salvation (see pp. 91-92)?
14. Can we be confident that someday we will be glorified? Support your answer with Scripture (see pp. 92-93).

Pondering the Principles

1. We groan as believers because we lament the evil we see in our lives. Do you groan over your sinfulness? Write a list of the weaknesses that you know are present in your life (for example: a quick temper, lustful thought patterns, a tendency to gossip). For each item on your list, ask yourself this question: *Do I groan over that weakness?* By asking that, you will find out how you really feel about the sins in your life. Begin to cultivate a genuine hatred for the sins in your life and a willingness to deal with them biblically.

2. Do you live in anticipation of eternal life with Christ? On a scale of 1 to 10, how strong would you rate your hope in your future salvation? Read the following verses: John 6:39; 10:28; Romans 8:35-39; 1 Peter 1:3-5; and Jude 1. What does each affirm about the security of our salvation? According to Titus 1:2, when did God promise believers eternal life? Will He revoke that promise? What did God give us as a pledge of His promise (2 Cor. 1:22; 5:5)? Read 2 Corinthians 4:18. Are you living in hope, or are you just focusing on your present circumstances? Don't allow anything to divert your focus from what awaits you in eternity, and don't fear losing your salvation. Thank God for the fact that "Christ in you [is] the hope of glory" (Col. 1:27).

7

The Spirit's Groans for Glory

Outline

Introduction
A. The Power That Keeps Us Secure
B. The Persons Who Keep Us Secure
   1. The Father
   2. The Son
   3. The Holy Spirit
C. The Promise to Keep Us Secure

Review
I.   The Incomparable Gain of Glory (vv. 17-18)
II. The Inexpressible Groans for Glory (vv. 19-27)
A. The Groan of Creation (vv. 19-22)
B. The Groan of Believers (vv. 23-25)

Lesson
C. The Groan of the Holy Spirit (vv. 26-27)
   1. His intercession for believers (v. 26)
   2. His interaction with God (v. 27)

Conclusion

Introduction

A. The Power That Keeps Us Secure

One of the most thrilling and hopeful verses in Scripture is 1 Peter 1:5, which says we "are kept by the power of God through faith unto salvation." As we've been learning in our study of Romans 8, our source of confidence, joy, and peace is our hope of eternal glory. We have the confidence that if we know Christ, we are kept by God's power.

First Peter 1:5 reminds us of something else we've been studying in Romans 8: our salvation is not yet complete. Romans 13:11 says, "Now is our salvation nearer than when we believed." There is a future dimension of salvation that will not be complete until we are glorified. Romans 8:29-30 says, "Whom he did foreknow, he also did predestinate to be conformed to the image of his Son. . . . Moreover, whom he did predestinate, them he also called; and whom he called, them he also justified; and whom he justified, them he also glorified." We who have been justified are waiting to be glorified.

Our being kept by God's power is known as the doctrine of eternal security or the perseverance of the saints. It's the reality behind the vernacular expression "Once saved, always saved." A more complete way of saying that is, "Once having entered salvation, we wait to see salvation complete." The apostle Paul put it this way: "He who began a good work in you will carry it on to completion until the day of Christ Jesus" (Phil. 1:6; NIV*).

The Puritan Thomas Watson said, "The exercise of grace may be hindered; as when the course of water is stopped . . . . Instead of grace working in the godly, corruption may work; instead of patience, murmuring; instead of heavenliness, earthliness. . . . Thus lively and vigorous may corruption be in the regenerate; they may fall into enormous sins. But though their grace may be drawn low, yet it is not drawn dry; though grace may be abated, it is not abolished. . . . Grace may suffer an eclipse, not a dissolution. . . . A believer may fall from some degrees of grace, but not from the state of grace" (*A Body of Divinity* [Carlisle, Pa.: The Banner of Truth Trust, 1986], pp. 280, 284-85).

B. The Persons Who Keep Us Secure

Why did Jesus say, "Of all that [the Father] hath given me I should lose nothing" (John 6:39)? Because when a person comes to Christ, the Lord secures his salvation for all eternity. In fact, the entire Trinity is involved in securing believers.

New International Version.

1. The Father

   a) 2 Corinthians 1:21-22—"He who establisheth us with you in Christ, and hath anointed us, is God, who hath also sealed us, and given the earnest of the Spirit in our hearts." The One who has established, anointed, and sealed us is God the Father. We are secure because He secures us.

   b) 2 Timothy 2:19—"The foundation of God standeth sure, having this seal, The Lord knoweth them that are his." Whoever belongs to God belongs to Him forever.

2. The Son

   First Corinthians 1:6-7 says, "The testimony of Christ was confirmed in you; so that ye come behind in no gift, waiting for the coming of our Lord Jesus Christ." We have received the testimony of Christ; now we wait His second coming. We have already been justified; now we are waiting to be glorified. In fact, Christ "shall . . . confirm you unto the end, that ye may be blameless in the day of our Lord Jesus Christ" (v. 8; cf. Col. 1:22; 1 Thess. 3:13). Christ Himself will confirm that we are blameless because we have trusted in Him as our Savior from sin.

3. The Holy Spirit

   Ephesians 1:13 says, "Ye were sealed with that Holy Spirit of promise." God guarantees our security by the work of the Holy Spirit. In 1 Thessalonians 5:23-24 Paul says, "The very God of peace sanctify you wholly; and I pray God your whole spirit and soul and body be preserved blameless unto the coming of our Lord Jesus Christ. Faithful is he that calleth you, who also will do it." We can be confident of God's ability to finish what He starts.

The teaching that a person can lose his or her salvation is foreign to Scripture. It disregards the work of the Father, the Son, and the Holy Spirit. The Father established that you are His forever. The Son confirms that and keeps you blameless. And the Spirit keeps you secure, stamping you with the divine seal. Those who have been saved are being kept saved (1 Pet. 1:5).

C. The Promise to Keep Us Secure

Hebrews 6:16 says, "Men verily swear by the greater, and an oath for confirmation is to them an end of all strife." When people make an oath, they swear by something greater than themselves. The Hebrew tradition was to swear by the Temple, God's name, or heaven. If two men had an argument and one took an oath, that would end the debate.

What's most impressive is when God Himself makes a vow: "God, willing more abundantly to show unto the heirs of promise the immutability of his counsel, confirmed it by an oath" (v. 17). God wanted to show "the heirs of promise" that He would never change His mind about their salvation. He confirmed His promise with an oath: "That by two immutable things, in which it was impossible for God to lie, we might have a strong consolation, who have fled for refuge to lay hold upon the hope before us, which hope we have as an anchor of the soul, both sure and steadfast, and which entereth into that within the veil" (vv. 18-19). When God promised salvation, He made an oath that bound Him. He cannot lie. We have strong consolation regarding our salvation because our anchor is the steadfast Word of God.

Review

The Holy Spirit frees us from sin, enables us to fulfill God's law, changes our nature, empowers us for victory, confirms our adoption, and guarantees our glory.

I.   THE INCOMPARABLE GAIN OF GLORY (vv. 17-18; see pp. 57-65)

II. THE INEXPRESSIBLE GROANS FOR GLORY (vv. 19-27)

A. The Groan of Creation (vv. 19-22; see pp. 72-79)

B. The Groan of Believers (vv. 23-25; see pp. 85-93)

C. The Groan of the Holy Spirit (vv. 26-27)

"Likewise, the Spirit also helpeth our infirmity; for we know not what we should pray for as we ought, but the Spirit himself maketh intercession for us with groanings which cannot be uttered. And he that searcheth the hearts knoweth what is the mind of the Spirit, because he maketh intercession for the saints according to the will of God."

He joins creation and believers in sighing over the fallen state of mankind and the universe. He longs for "the glorious liberty of the children of God" (v. 21) and "the manifestation of the sons of God" (v. 19).

It's difficult to understand the concept of the Holy Spirit's groanings, but it does offer immediate encouragement: we who groan under the weight of our fallenness and wait for our bodies to be redeemed are not alone—the Holy Spirit groans over the same thing. When we lament with Paul, "Oh, wretched man that I am! Who shall deliver me from the body of this death?" (Rom. 7:24), the Holy Spirit groans with us because He understands.

The Spirit Doesn't Groan in Tongues

Charismatics say that when Paul talked about "groanings which cannot be uttered," he was referring to speaking in tongues. However, it is the Holy Spirit who is speaking in Romans 8:26—not people. Moreover, the Spirit doesn't really speak, for the groanings He emits "cannot be uttered." Finally, nothing in the context of Romans 8:26-27 is related to the issue of speaking in tongues.

Romans 8:26 begins with "likewise." Just as creation and believers groan, the Spirit also groans. God is on our side. Some Christians go through life expecting to be punished by God for every little thing they do wrong. Although it's true that God chastens His own (Heb. 12:6), our humanness is as much a concern of the Spirit as it is to us. The Holy Spirit wants us to get rid of our sin as much as we do. That's a comforting thought. The only time we should expect God's discipline is when we are happy with our sin and don't repent of it. But as long as we groan for our deliverance, then God's Spirit will groan with us. He wants us to be set free from the flesh and given full salvation.

1. His intercession for believers (v. 26)

Our security is a result of God's plan, Christ's gift, and the Holy Spirit's ongoing work in us. We know our salvation is eternal, but we have to be kept saved (1 Pet. 1:5). That is a divine work of the Spirit and the Lord Jesus Christ.

a) It's in conjunction with Christ

In Luke 22:31 Jesus says to Peter, "Simon, Simon, behold, Satan hath desired to have you, that he may sift you as wheat; but I have prayed for thee, that thy faith fail not." On the surface it might appear as if Jesus wasn't trusting in God's sovereign plan of salvation. While it's true salvation is eternal, it is still carried out by the Son's intercession. You can't separate God's plan from the work of Christ and the Spirit. The Lord said He would pray that Peter's faith would remain. Would God answer that prayer? Jesus predicted He would, saying to Peter, "When thou art converted [when you overcome the trial], strengthen thy brethren" (v. 32).

God planned the believer's security; the Son and the Spirit carry it out. If They didn't, God's plan would be nullified. If for one moment Jesus stopped cleansing you from your sin, you would go to hell—even if you had already put your faith in Christ. That's why 1 John 1:9 says, "If we confess our sins, he is faithful and just to forgive us our sins, and to cleanse us from all unrighteousness." There must be constant intercession on our behalf by the Son and the Spirit. Romans 8:26 says, "The Spirit also helpeth our infirmity." We can't keep ourselves saved—we are too weak.

Can't we pray for ourselves? We could try, but the problem is we don't know precisely what to pray for. We struggle with sin and the weakness of our flesh, and we don't know what the future holds. Only the Lord knows when something will

100

happen to us, just as He knew that Peter was about to be tested (Luke 22:31). Peter didn't know what was going to happen; he could have walked blindly into the trial and been overcome by it. So the Lord prayed for Peter even before the trial occurred.

The Savior and Spirit intercede for us because we can't maintain our redemption. The Spirit helps our weaknesses. He doesn't just help us in our weak prayers; He helps us in our mortal, sinful state.

While many acknowledge that believers are secure forever because of God's sovereign plan, they miss the corresponding truth that eternal security rests also on the intercessory work of the Son and the Spirit. Peter was safe because Christ prayed for him. We should be grateful that Christ also helps us in our weaknesses.

Hebrews 7:25 says, "[Christ] is able also to save them to the uttermost that come unto God by him, seeing he ever liveth to make intercession for them." What does it mean to be saved "to the uttermost"? To be saved to the limit—from the moment of salvation to our glorification. Verse 26 continues, "For such an high priest was fitting for us." Without the intercessory work of Christ, we would never get to heaven.

Not only does Christ intercede for us, but the Holy Spirit intercedes for us as well. We have a faithful High Priest in heaven, and a faithful High Priest in our hearts: "The Spirit himself maketh intercession for us" (Rom. 8:26). The Greek word translated "intercession" is the same one used in Hebrews 7:25 in reference to Christ. We can't pray for ourselves effectively because we don't know how to protect ourselves in the midst of spiritual conflict. We need help from the Savior in heaven and the Spirit on earth.

In God We Trust

According to 2 Corinthians 12 Paul prayed three times for the Lord to remove "a thorn in the flesh" (v. 7). But the Lord didn't remove it. In Philippians 4:11 Paul says, "I have learned, in whatever state I am . . . to be content." He learned what all of us should know: we really don't know how to pray for ourselves. When we suffer, we pray, "Lord, get rid of my suffering. I've learned my lesson. I don't need to suffer anymore." We fail to consider that a worse fate might befall us if it weren't for the suffering God allows us to endure. Trust the Lord. We don't know what's best for us, but God does.

b) It's a divine rescue mission

How does the Spirit intercede for us? The Greek word translated "intercession" is a multiple compound word: two prepositions attached to a verb. It speaks of rescuing someone in trouble who has no resources to escape. Satan knows we are kept by the power of Christ and the Spirit. He wars against Their power with all the hosts of hell in an attempt to debilitate their work of keeping believers. Christ isn't in heaven watching everything fall into place; He is continuously working to uphold all things. The Spirit of God isn't finished, either. He didn't stop working when the age of miracles ended after the apostolic era. He continues in marvelous, supernatural ways to uphold believers.

The Holy Spirit intercedes by rescuing us when we have no resource for rescuing ourselves. Notice the emphasis in verse 26: "the Spirit himself [Gk., *autos*]." It is *His* work.

The Content of the Spirit's Groans

The Spirit groans "with groanings which cannot be uttered" (v. 26). Those are divine sighs by the Spirit as He prays to the Father for the glorification of fallen creatures who would never be glorified if it weren't for His intercession. The Spirit understands our weaknesses: He knows that we sin and that we don't know how to pray to defend ourselves. He yearns for us to be like Christ.

The intertrinitarian groanings of the Holy Spirit have content, but they transcend language. They are "groanings which cannot be uttered." We don't know what He is saying, but we can be sure He is praying for us.

c) It brings sure results

No believer will ever be lost to God. The only thing that could keep you from glorification would be if Christ could no longer sit at the right hand of God and intercede for you, or if the Spirit could no longer cry out before God on your behalf. But that won't happen since God is eternal. Paul said "Work out your own salvation with fear and trembling. For it is God who worketh in you both to will and to do of his good pleasure" (Phil. 2:12-13). The Spirit works in you to bring about God's perfect will. Paul called that "the supply of the Spirit of Jesus Christ" (Phil. 1:19). God supplies you with all you need to endure life and make it to glory.

d) It's an ongoing ministry

The Holy Spirit seals us by His constant intercession on our behalf. In the Bible a seal is a sign of authenticity. If someone wanted to prove something was real, he would put a seal on it. A seal was also used to signify a completed transaction. When someone sold a plot of land, a seal confirmed the agreement between the buyer and the seller (e.g., Jer. 32:7-15). That's similar to pink slips that verify car ownership. Scripture also refers to a seal as a sign of authority. When someone acted as a representative for a monarch, he would carry the monarch's seal with him. That proved he represented the monarch's authority.

Primarily, though, Scripture uses the seal as a sign of security. When it says we are sealed with the Spirit (Eph. 1:13), that means we are secure. The best Old Testament illustration of that appears in Daniel 6: "The king commanded, and they brought Daniel, and cast him into the den of lions. Now the king spoke and said unto Daniel, Thy God, whom thou servest continually, he will deliver thee. And a stone was brought, and laid upon the mouth of the den; and the king sealed it with his own signet, and with the signet of his lords, that the purpose might not be changed concerning Daniel" (vv. 16-17). When you are sealed with the Spirit, that means God's purpose in salvation can never be changed. The seal of our security is the Holy

103

Spirit Himself, who assures us by His ongoing intercessory work. That is why He is called the "Holy Spirit of promise" (Eph. 1:13). He is the reason the promise of ultimate redemption is fulfilled.

2. His interaction with God (v. 27)

    a) God listens to the Holy Spirit (v. 27a)

Romans 8:27 says, "He that searcheth the hearts knoweth what is the mind of the Spirit." Do you know who searches our hearts?

    (1) 1 Samuel 16:7—"Man looketh on the outward appearance, but the Lord looketh on the heart."

    (2) 1 Kings 8:39—"Thou, even thou only, knowest the hearts of all the children of men."

    (3) 1 Chronicles 28:9—"The Lord searcheth all hearts, and understandeth all the imaginations of the thoughts."

    (4) Psalm 139:1-2—"O Lord, thou hast searched me, and known me. Thou knowest my downsitting and mine uprising; thou understandest my thought afar off."

    (5) Proverbs 15:11—"Sheol [the grave] and destruction are before the Lord; how much more, then, the hearts of the children of men!"

    (6) Acts 1:24—"Thou, Lord, . . . knowest the hearts of all men."

    (7) 1 Corinthians 4:5—"[The Lord] will bring to light the hidden things of darkness, and will make manifest the counsels of the hearts."

    (8) Hebrews 4:13—"Neither is there any creature that is not manifest in his sight, but all things are naked and opened unto the eyes of him with whom we have to do."

God searches our hearts. Romans 8:26 says that the Holy Spirit prays for us, and verse 27 says that God hears: "He that searcheth the hearts knoweth what is the mind of the Spirit." In the intertrinitarian communion taking place amidst the Spirit's groanings, God hears the Holy Spirit's prayers.

b) The Holy Spirit prays for God's will (v. 27*b*)

God knows "what is the mind of the Spirit, because [the Spirit] maketh intercession for the saints according to the will of God" (v. 27). You may not know the precise will of God or exactly how to pray, but the Spirit knows. Jude says we are to pray in the Spirit (v. 20). That doesn't mean we become ecstatic but that we pray according to the will of God. The Lord knows what the Spirit is praying because everything He prays for is in accord with God's will. There is perfect harmony within the Trinity.

The Holy Spirit and the Son intercede for us according to God's will. God hears and understands Their intercession, and responds to it. We are kept by the Spirit and the Son's interceding ministries. Anyone who believes a Christian can lose his or her salvation is questioning the power of the Spirit and the Savior.

Conclusion

Romans 8:28 tells us what happens as a result of the Spirit's intercessory work: we have the assurance "that all things work together for good to them that love God, to them who are the called according to his purpose." God's purpose is to bring us to glory and conform us to Christ. Everything works toward that end because of the intercessory work of the Spirit. All things work together for our good not because we are wonderful and have the ability to make things work out that way but because God leads us to glory and the Spirit keeps us on that path by His intercessory work in our hearts. That is the guarantee of glory.

Focusing on the Facts

1. What is a more accurate way of saying, "Once saved, always saved" (see p. 96)?
2. What does God do in securing Christians (2 Cor. 1:21-22; 2 Tim. 2:19; see p. 97)?

3. What does 1 Corinthians 1:8 indicate about Christ's involvement in securing our salvation (see p. 97)?
4. What does 1 Thessalonians 5:23-24 say in regard to the security of our salvation (see p. 97)?
5. What significant promise appears in Hebrews 6:16-19 (see p. 98)?
6. How can the concept of the Spirit's groanings encourage us (see p. 99)?
7. How do we know the Holy Spirit's groanings aren't a reference to speaking in tongues (see p. 99)?
8. Even though God planned that salvation be eternal, why are we dependent on intercessory prayer (cf. Luke 22:31-32; see p. 100)?
9. Why can't we pray to keep ourselves saved (see pp. 100-101)?
10. What corresponding truth do people often miss about eternal security (see p. 101)?
11. What does "intercession" mean in Romans 8:26 (see p. 102)?
12. Discuss the content of the Holy Spirit's groans (see p. 102).
13. What kind of interaction do we see among the Trinity in Romans 8:27 (see pp. 104-5)?
14. What happens as a result of the Spirit's intercessory work (Rom. 8:28; see p. 105)?

Pondering the Principles

1. Believers have two intercessors: Christ and the Holy Spirit. Christ is our High Priest in heaven (Heb. 8:1), and the Holy Spirit intercedes for us in our hearts (Rom. 8:26-27). The intercessory ministries of the Savior and the Spirit reveal the genuine concern They have for all believers. Do you show the same kind of concern for other Christians in your prayers? Have you ever prayed earnestly for another believer on a regular basis? Pick one Christian you know, and pray for him or her every day for the next two weeks. Seek to minister to fellow believers in that way on a regular basis.

2. Romans 8 says that the Holy Spirit prays for us "according to the will of God" (v. 27). That is a marvelous ministry, especially when considering that we don't always know what is best for us. Meditate on this: When you pray for yourself, do you pray in accord with the will of God? Write a list of the things you have prayed for recently. If God were to pray for you, would He pray for the same things? Write a list of what you think He would pray for. What can you learn about your prayer life when you compare the two lists?

Begin to cultivate a regular habit of praying in accord with God's will.

8

The Promise of Security—Part 1

Outline

Lesson
I. The Extent (v. 28b)
    A. Good Things Work for Our Good
        1. God's attributes
        2. God's promises
        3. God's Word
        4. Prayer
        5. Angels
        6. Fellow Christians
    B. Bad Things Work for Our Good
        1. Suffering
            a) Reasons for suffering
            b) Examples of suffering
            c) Benefits of suffering
        2. Temptation
        3. Sin
            a) The sins of others
            b) Our own sins

Conclusion

Lesson

If the whole of Scripture were a feast for the soul, Romans 8 would be the main dish. The wonder of this chapter is summarized in verse 28: "We know that all things work together for good to them that love God, to them who are the called according to his purpose." That is the most glorious promise imaginable and deserves our close attention.

Let's examine four elements of the promise of security in verse 28: the extent, recipients, source, and certainty of that promise.

I. THE EXTENT (v. 28*b*)

"All things work together for good."

Nothing could be more reassuring than that. Nothing could bring more hope, joy, trust, confidence, happiness, and freedom "to them that love God" than knowing their pain, problems, and trials all "work together for good."

"All things" tells us there is no limit to what works out for our good. Romans 8:28 is not limited to "all suffering," "all trouble," "all good things," or "all righteousness." Neither is it saying that all things are in themselves good. Many things are bad, but even they "work together for good." No matter what happens to us, it works out for our good.

The Greek word translated "good" in Romans 8:28 (*agathon*) refers to something that is morally or inherently good. Another common Greek word translated "good" is *kalos*, which means "good on the outside" or "nice to look at." *Agathos* refers to what is intrinsically good, not to what is just superficially good. In fact, it refers even to things that don't look good, yet are inherently good. Paul's use of *agathon* indicates the purest, truest kind of goodness.

In saying all things work together for good, I believe Paul had two things in mind: our current circumstances and our future glorification. No matter what happens in our lives, God will work things out to produce something immediately and ultimately beneficial for us. And since everything in our lives ultimately works for our good, nothing could ever cause us to lose our salvation.

Deuteronomy 8:15-16 tells us God worked out difficult circumstances for the good of the Israelites: "[God] led thee through that great and terrible wilderness, wherein were fiery serpents, and scorpions, and drought, where there was no water; who brought thee forth water out of the rock of flint; who fed thee in the wilderness with manna, which thy fathers knew not, that he might humble thee, and that he might test thee, to do thee good at thy latter end." God didn't send Israel through forty difficult years in the wilderness to do them evil; He did it to refine them. Everything ultimately works for the good of God's children.

That doesn't happen automatically, however. The Holy Spirit and the Son are constantly interceding on our behalf (Rom. 8:26-27; Heb. 7:25).

A. Good Things Work for Our Good

1. God's attributes

God's power supports us in the midst of trouble. As Deuteronomy 33:27 says, "The eternal God is thy refuge, and underneath are the everlasting arms." God supported Daniel when he was in a lions' den (Dan. 6:21-23), Jonah when he was in a fish's belly (Jonah 1:17–2:10), and three Hebrew men when they were thrown into a furnace (Dan. 3:12-28). The apostle Paul said that God's strength is on display in our weaknesses (2 Cor. 12:9). He infuses us with His power. Christ told the apostles, "Ye shall receive power, after the Holy Spirit is come upon you" (Acts 1:8).

His wisdom and goodness are also at our disposal. Romans 2:4 says that the goodness of God leads us to repentance, which certainly is a good end.

2. God's promises

When we repent of our sin, we are reminded that the Lord God is "merciful and gracious" (Ex. 34:6). When we have been disobedient, we can remember Hosea 14:4, where God says He will heal our backsliding, or Micah 7:18, which says, "Who is a God like Thee, who pardons iniquity?" (NASB).

Psalm 91:15 reassures us that God is with us in all our troubles. Philippians 4:19 promises, "God shall supply all your need." As David said, "I [have] not seen the righteous forsaken, nor his seed begging bread" (Ps. 37:25).

3. God's Word

The Bible works for our good. Paul told the elders of the church at Ephesus, "I commend you to God, and to the word of his grace, which is able to build you up, and to give you an inheritance among all them who are sanctified" (Acts 20:32).

4. Prayer

   Prayer releases God's power in our lives.

5. Angels

   Hebrews 1:14 says that angels are "ministering spirits, sent forth to minister for them who shall be heirs of salvation."

6. Fellow Christians

   Paul said to the Corinthian church, "[We] are helpers of your joy" (2 Cor. 1:24). As Christians we are to help one another. That's why Hebrews 10:24 says, "Let us consider one another to provoke unto love and to good works."

While God's attributes, God's promises, the Bible, prayer, angels, and other believers work for our good, Paul was not focusing on those things in Romans 8:28.

B. Bad Things Work for Our Good

That's not to say bad things *are* good—bad things are always evil. We don't want to redefine them as good and invent a new theology. Sin is sin, evil is evil, and that won't ever change. Bad things are never good, but God uses them to work for our good. God's sovereignty extends over both bad things and good things. He can overrule the vilest things and work them out to our good. If you are in God's family, you can be confident that no matter what happens to you, God will work it out for your good now and in future glory.

Let's look at three categories of bad things that work for our good.

1. Suffering

   Suffering is a result of the curse. If sin had not been introduced into the world, there would be no suffering. There would be no pain, sorrow, or death. Although suffering itself is not evil, it is the result of an evil world.

   In Ruth 1:21 Naomi says, "The Almighty hath afflicted me." Job, in the midst of terrible circumstances, said,

"The Lord gave, and the Lord hath taken away" (Job 1:21). God said of the Israelites, "I [will] acknowledge those who are carried away captive of Judah, whom I have sent out of this place into the land of the Chaldeans for their good" (Jer. 24:5). Just as God allowed the Israelites to suffer for their good, so He is using our suffering for our good.

a) Reasons for suffering

Sometimes our suffering is God's chastening for sin. But not all suffering is the result of sin. Sometimes God allows us to suffer so that He can refine us. Suffering purifies us as fire refines gold (1 Pet. 1:7). It also has a way of making us focus on God.

Although suffering has many purposes, God uses it all to achieve good results. James said, "My brethren, count it all joy when ye fall into various trials, knowing this, that the testing of your faith worketh patience" (James 1:2-3). Peter said, "After ye have suffered awhile, [the Lord will] make you perfect" (1 Peter 5:10). God uses suffering to help us grow spiritually. Through it we learn kindness, sympathy, compassion, patience, and gentleness. It leads us to look to God, trust Him, and depend on His power, grace, and mercy.

b) Examples of suffering

(1) Joseph

Joseph's brothers threw him into a pit and then sold him to some men on their way to Egypt (Gen. 37:20-28). Later he was imprisoned (Gen. 39:20). God, however, worked out all his suffering for good. Joseph interpreted a dream for Pharaoh and warned of a coming famine (Gen. 41:1-44). As a result Pharaoh made Joseph prime minister of Egypt. If that had not happened, Joseph's brothers would not have received grain from Egypt when they went there to buy it (Gen. 42:25; 44:1). Joseph sympathetically gave them what they needed. God worked out the evil done to Joseph to for his good and the good of those around him (Gen. 50:20).

113

(2) Manasseh

The Assyrians took evil King Manasseh of Judah captive. Manasseh's suffering brought about a good result: "When he was in affliction, he besought the Lord, his God, and humbled himself greatly before the God of his fathers" (2 Chron. 33:12). The Lord responded to Manasseh's humility.

Suffering can bring us closer to God and purge the sin in our lives. It teaches us what other people go through when they suffer, enabling us to minister more compassionately to them (2 Cor. 1:3-4).

(3) Job

Job lost everything. The only thing he didn't lose was his wife, but she didn't help him much (Job 2:9). His barns were destroyed, his cattle were stolen, and his children killed (1:14-19). Job had sores all over his body (2:7). Yet after all the suffering he endured, he was still able to say to the Lord, "I have heard of thee by the hearing of the ear, but now mine eye seeth thee. Wherefore I abhor myself, and repent in dust and ashes" (42:5-6). Although his suffering cost him everything, God gave him back more than he ever lost (42:10).

(4) Paul

The apostle Paul was burdened by "a thorn in the flesh" (2 Cor. 12:7). He asked God to remove it, but came to realize that thorn enabled him to see God's power through his weakness. When Paul was afflicted with blindness on the Damascus Road, it worked for his good in drawing him to Christ.

c) Benefits of suffering

(1) It teaches us to hate sin

Puritan Thomas Watson wrote an entire book on Romans 8:28 (*All Things for Good*, originally titled *A Divine Cordial* [Carlisle, Pa.: The Banner of

114

Truth Trust, 1986]). He observed that Martin Luther said he never understood the imprecatory psalms until he himself had suffered. Luther didn't know how David felt when crying out for vengeance on his enemies until he too was in affliction. Watson commented, "Affliction teaches what sin is. . . . A sick-bed often teaches more than a sermon. We can best see the ugly visage of sin in the glass of affliction" (p. 27).

When Jesus went to Lazarus's tomb, He "groaned in the spirit, and was troubled" (John 11:33). He agonized over the tears, pain, and sorrow that sin and death bring. When you experience suffering, you learn to hate the sin that brings it about.

(2) It helps us see our own evil

When you suffer, you find out what is really going on inside you. When everything is fine it's easy to feel pious. But as soon as things collapse and troubles come your way, it's even easier to shake your fist at God. You can become impatient and begin to doubt God. That's when you find out if you really trust Him. Suffering will expose any evil in your heart.

(3) It drives us to God

In prosperity the heart is easily divided. That's why God warned the Israelites not to forget Him when they went into the Promised Land (Deut. 6:10-13). Suffering forces us to stop focusing on the world. When everything in your life is great, you're apt to be preoccupied with your house, car, job, business, and wardrobe. But suppose one of your children became terminally ill. That would change your values and drive you to God. That is a good response to a bad situation.

(4) It conforms us to Christ

When we suffer, we enter into "the fellowship of [Christ's] sufferings" (Phil. 3:10). Suffering helps us identify with Him. That's why Paul

115

was happy to say, "I bear in my body the marks of the Lord Jesus" (Gal. 6:17). He knew what it was like to be beaten up and pummeled by rocks and rods. He identified with the reproach of Christ, bearing it in his own body. Suffering helps us to better understand Christ's heart, pain, and suffering. It brings us into deeper intimacy with the One who suffered for us.

(5) It drives out sin

Suffering is a fire that burns away our dross and reveals the pure gold and silver. As Job said, "When he hath tested me, I shall come forth as gold" (Job 23:10). Suffering drives out sin. Zechariah 13:8-9 tells us God will use the terrors of the Tribulation to refine the nation of Israel in the end times.

(6) It reveals that we are sons of God

Hebrews 12:6-8 says, "Whom the Lord loveth he chasteneth, and scourgeth every son whom he receiveth. If ye endure chastening, God dealeth with you as with sons; for what son is he whom the father chasteneth not? But if ye be without chastisement, of which all are partakers, then are ye [illegitimate], and not sons." When you suffer because the Lord is refining you, be glad because He is making you into the child you ought to be.

I have four children. My wife and I disciplined them because we wanted to refine them into the people the Lord would have them to be. They have no question that I'm their father because they know I'm the source of discipline, and they also know the loving purpose behind it. I hope that is true about your family. God disciplines His children to refine them. When you suffer because God is chastening you, praise God for that sign that you're His child. Job 5:17 says, "Happy is the man whom God correcteth."

The psalmist said, "Before I was afflicted I went astray, but now have I kept thy word. . . . It is good for me that I have been afflicted, that I might learn

116

thy statutes. . . . I know, O Lord, that thy judgments are right, and that thou in faithfulness hast afflicted me" (Ps. 119:67, 71, 75). Suffering is a direct result of sin in the world. But God overrules it for the good of believers.

2. Temptation

   a) It makes us prayerful

   Temptation drives us to God in prayer. When an animal sees a hunter, he runs for safety. When a believer sees the devil coming with temptation, he should flee into the presence of God that God might overrule it.

   b) It devastates our pride

   When you struggle with sin and temptation, you see who you really are and realize you have no reason to be proud of yourself. You find out how weak you really are.

   c) It enables us to help others

   Satan tempted our Lord three times in the wilderness (Matt. 4:1-11; Luke 4:1-13). God recorded that event to show us how Christ handled Satan's attacks. Hebrews 4:15-16 says, "We have not an high priest who cannot be touched with the feeling of our infirmities, but was in all points tempted like as we are, yet without sin. Let us, therefore, come boldly unto the throne of grace, that we may obtain mercy, and find grace to help in time of need." Because Christ experienced temptation, He understands what we go through and is therefore able to help us in our struggles. That enables us to help others in their struggles.

   d) It makes us depend on Christ

   When we struggle with temptation, we are forced to lean on the strength of Christ. That's similar to running into God's presence. The apostle Paul lived in utter dependence on Christ's strength (Phil. 4:13).

e) It makes us desire heaven

Have you ever wanted to get away from the world? I'm sure you have—especially when you struggle with temptation. Like Paul you may cry out, "The good that I would, I do not; but the evil which I would not, that I do. . . . Oh, wretched man that I am!" (Rom. 7:19, 24). At times like that you'll long for heaven and glory, saying with Paul, "To me to live is Christ, and to die is gain. . . . I am in a strait between two, having a desire to depart and to be with Christ, which is far better" (Phil. 1:21, 23).

3. Sin

Romans 8:28 declares that "all things work together for good," and that includes sin. No matter what happens to us as Christians, God will ultimately work it out for our good. Now that doesn't lessen the ugliness of sin or the beauty of holiness. Sin deserves eternal hell. But God in His greatness overrules it for the believer's good.

a) The sins of others

When we see sin in other people, we sense a holy indignation against it. That leads us to be stronger in our opposition to sin, as does seeing what sin does to other people. I also become more thankful for the sins the Lord has delivered me from.

b) Our own sins

God is so powerful that He overrules the sins we commit. The difference between a Christian and a non-Christian is not that the Christian doesn't sin, but that ultimately his sin and the consequences of it are eliminated. In the interim, however, the Christian will experience temporary chastisement from the heavenly Father. Because Christ already paid the penalty for our sin, God overrules the ultimate consequence of damnation (Rom. 6:23).

Our sins work for our good by making us look to glory. As we studied earlier, our sinful flesh groans for the day of its redemption (Rom. 8:23). When we recognize sin in us, we cry out for deliverance.

Another thing we do is run to God to confess our sin and repent of it. That brings us into communion with Him.

Conclusion

All things work together for our good because of what God teaches us through them. That good is not just temporal but eternal. All the attacks we receive from hell and all the mistakes we make can never alter the ultimate glory that is ours in Christ. Romans 8:29-30 says, "Whom [God] did foreknow, he also did predestinate to be conformed to the image of his Son, that he might be the firstborn among many brethren. Moreover, whom he did predestinate, them he also called; and whom he called, them he also justified; and whom he justified, them he also glorified." Our salvation is a sure thing!

All things work out for the believer's good because God has predetermined that to happen. We who were chosen in Him before the foundation of the world will become like Jesus Christ no matter what. God doesn't merely promise that temporal good will come out of difficult situations; He also affirms that all the bad things of this world can't keep us from glorification and heaven. What a great truth!

Focusing on the Facts

1. Is there any limit on the wonderful promise in Romans 8:28? How do we know (see p. 110)?
2. What is significant about Paul's use of *agathon* in Romans 8:28 (see p. 110)?
3. Does the working out of everything for our good happen automatically? Explain (see p. 111).
4. Give some examples of how God's power worked out for the good of His children (see p. 111).
5. What are some promises from God that work out for our good (see p. 111)?
6. Can bad things be good? Explain (see p. 112).
7. Why do believers suffer? What can we learn through suffering (see pp. 112-13)?
8. How did Joseph's suffering turn out for his good and the good of those around him (see pp. 113-14)?
9. What effect did suffering have on King Manasseh of Judah (2 Chron. 33:12; see p. 114)?

10. List and explain the ways that we can benefit from suffering (see pp. 114-16).
11. What did the author of Psalm 119 say about suffering (vv. 67, 71, 75; see pp. 116-17)?
12. How can temptation work out for our good (see pp. 117-18)?
13. How do we know Jesus is able to help us when we are tempted (Heb. 4:15-16; see p. 117)?
14. How can the sins of other people work for our good (see p. 118)?
15. How can our sins work for our good (see pp. 118-19)?

Pondering the Principles

1. Paul knew God would always work things out for the good of His people because he knew how God had dealt with Israel in the past. Read Joshua 24:1-15 and Nehemiah 9:7-32. What evidence do you see of God's care for the Israelites? What difficult circumstances has God worked out for your good that show His care for you? How did He use the suffering you endured for your benefit? Thank God for all the good and bad things you know of that have worked out for your good. Praise Him for working out those things for your good in the future.

2. Read Deuteronomy 6:10-13. Are you in prosperous circumstances now that could distract you from seeking God wholeheartedly? Think about all the things that frequently occupy your mind. Are any of them taking up more time than they should? How much of your time is devoted to communing with God and studying His Word? Don't wait for difficult circumstances to arise before you run to God for help; seek Him constantly. Instead of becoming complacent when things are going well, praise God for all the blessings He has bestowed on you.

3. When you are tempted, what is your usual response? Do you think God is pleased with how you handle temptation? Review the section on the reasons that temptation works out for our good (see pp. 9-10). Are all those elements present in your response to temptation? Try to think of specific examples of when you responded in one or more of those ways to a temptation. What effect did your responses have on your relationship with God? On your growth as a Christian? Looking back at what has happened in your life when you have been tempted, can you wholeheartedly thank

God for how He has worked out things for your good? Don't ever become discouraged when you are tempted; rather, look for how you can benefit from your situation. Thank the Lord that all things truly do "work together for good to them that love God" (Rom. 8:28).

9
The Promise of Security—Part 2

Outline

Review
I. The Extent (v. 28b)

Lesson
II. The Recipients (v. 28c)
  A. Those Who Love God
    1. The motive of our love for God
    2. The degree of our love for God
    3. The characteristics of our love for God
  B. Those Who Are Called
III. The Source (v. 28d)
IV. The Certainty (v. 28a)

Conclusion

Review

Romans 8 is like a mountain range with many peaks. Verse 28 is the highest peak and most majestic mountain in the range. It sums up the security of the believer in a way no other portion of Scripture does: "We know that all things work together for good to them that love God, to them who are the called according to his purpose."

I. THE EXTENT (v. 28b; see pp. 110-19)

"All things work together for good."

All things work together ultimately for the believer's good, and that includes suffering, temptation, and sin. Things that

123

are in themselves bad are overruled by God for our good in the present and in the future.

The ultimate future good is our eternal glory. Verses 29-30 speak of our moving toward glorification and verses 23-25 refer to the redemption of our bodies. We await the ultimate glory of a home in heaven in the presence of Christ. Everything happening to us now moves us toward that glory.

Nothing can overrule God's plan. Verses 29-30 describe an inevitable process: God foreknew us, predestinated us, called us, justified us, and will glorify us. Verse 31 summarizes: "If God be for us, who can be against us?" Since God has done so much to guarantee our glory, who can overrule His work? Can death, life, angels, principalities, powers, things present, things to come, height, depth, or any creature withstand God (vv. 38-39)? The obvious answer is no. None of those things individually or collectively can change God's plan for our ultimate good.

Lesson

II. THE RECIPIENTS (v. 28c)

"To them that love God, to them who are the called."

All things work together for good, but not for everyone. Two phrases identify the recipients of that promise: "them that love God" and "them who are the called."

A. Those Who Love God

In Scripture Christians are alternately called children of God, sons of God, believers, true worshipers, and saints. Here they are identified as "them that love God." From our perspective, we are "them that love God." From God's perspective, we are "them who are the called."

Nothing is more indicative of our character as Christians than our love for God. "Them that love God" is a wonderful way to describe redeemed people.

124

1. The motive of our love for God

Believers are often described in the Bible as those who love God.

a) Exodus 20:5-6—"Thou shalt not bow down thyself to [idols], nor serve them; for I, the Lord thy God, am a jealous God, visiting the iniquity of the fathers upon the children unto the third and fourth generation of them that hate me; and showing mercy unto thousands of them that love me, and keep my commandments." Humanity is divided into two groups: those who hate God (v. 5) and those who love Him (v. 6).

b) 1 Corinthians 2:9—"Eye hath not seen, nor ear heard, neither have entered into the heart of man, the things which God hath prepared for them that love him."

c) 1 Corinthians 8:3—"If any man love God, the same is known of him."

d) James 1:12—"Blessed is the man that endureth temptation; for when he is tried, he shall receive the crown of life, which the Lord hath promised to them that love him."

2. The degree of our love for God

Why does the Bible frequently identify Christians as those who love God? Why doesn't Paul identify believers in Romans 8:28 as "those who are saved" or "those who are the children of God"? I think Paul was affirming a basic element in salvation: true saving faith goes beyond mere belief. James 2:19 says, "Thou believest that there is one God; thou doest well. The demons also believe, and tremble." True salvation produces lovers of God.

a) Ephesians 6:23-24—"Peace be to the brethren, and love with faith, from God, the Father, and the Lord Jesus Christ. Grace be with all them that love our Lord Jesus Christ in sincerity." Grace belongs only to those who genuinely love God and Christ.

b) Luke 6:46—"Why call ye me, Lord, Lord, and do not the things which I say?" If we are not obedient, our profession of faith means nothing because obedience is the fruit of love.

c) Luke 7:46-47—Jesus said to a Pharisee, "My head with oil thou didst not anoint. But this woman hath anointed my feet with ointment. Wherefore, I say unto thee, Her sins, which are many, are forgiven; for she loved much. But to whom little is forgiven, the same loveth little." If we have been forgiven much, we will love much. The mark of a true believer is that he loves God very much.

d) John 15:13-14—"Greater love hath no man than this, that a man lay down his life for his friends. Ye are my friends, if ye do whatever I command you."

e) 2 Corinthians 5:14—Paul said, "The love of Christ constraineth us."

A true believer is someone who loves God and the Lord Jesus Christ. Realize, however, that in this life we will never love God as much as we ought. That's why Paul said, "This I pray, that your love may abound yet more and more in knowledge and in all judgment" (Phil. 1:9).

3. The characteristics of our love for God

How can you know if you truly love God?

a) A true Christian praises God's glory

A person with a true love for God is thrilled with who He is. Psalm 18:1-3 says, "I will love thee, O Lord, my strength. The Lord is my rock, and my fortress, and my deliverer; my God, my strength, in whom I will trust; my shield, and the horn of my salvation, and my high tower. I will call upon the Lord, who is worthy to be praised."

b) A true Christian trusts in God's power

Psalm 31:23-24 says, "Oh, love the Lord, all ye his saints; for the Lord preserveth the faithful, and plentifully rewardeth the proud doer. Be of good courage, and he shall strengthen your heart, all ye that hope in the Lord."

126

c) A true Christian seeks communion with God

Love seeks to commune with the object of its devotion. David said, "O God, thou art my God, early will I seek thee; my soul thirsteth for thee, my flesh longeth for thee in a dry and thirsty land, where no water is, to see thy power and thy glory, as I have seen thee in the sanctuary. Because thy loving-kindness is better than life, my lips shall praise thee" (Ps. 63:1-3). Another psalmist wrote, "My soul longeth, yea, even fainteth for the courts of the Lord; my heart and my flesh cry out for the living God. Yea, the sparrow hath found an house, and the swallow a nest for herself, where she may lay her young, even thine altars, O Lord of hosts, my King and my God. Blessed are they who dwell in thy house; they will be still praising thee" (Ps. 84:2-4).

d) A true Christian enjoys God's peace

People who don't have a love relationship with God are anxious. But when a person finds the perfect object of his love, he will rest. Thus when we come to know God and experience His love, we enter into a peace like no other. Psalm 119:165 says, "Great peace have they who love thy law."

e) A true Christian is sensitive to God

When God is hurt over something, a true believer will also feel that hurt. It's like feeling the hurt of another family member. David reflected such devotion when he said to God, "The zeal of thine house hath eaten me up; and the reproaches of those who reproached thee are fallen upon me" (Ps. 69:9). When God was dishonored, that hurt David.

f) A true Christian loves what God loves

What does God love? David said, "Thou hast magnified thy word above all thy name" (Ps. 138:2). God loves His Word; the person who loves God also loves His Word. As the psalmist said, "The law of thy mouth is better unto me than thousands of gold and silver. . . . Oh, how love I thy law! It is my meditation all the day. . . . How sweet are thy words unto my taste! Yea, sweeter than honey to my mouth" (Ps. 119:72, 97, 103).

g) A true Christian loves whom God loves

First John 5:1-2 says, "Whosoever believeth that Jesus is the Christ is born of God; and everyone that loveth him that begot loveth him also that is begotten of him. By this we know that we love the children of God, when we love God, and keep his commandments." If you are a child of God you will love Him, keep His commandments, and love His children.

h) A true Christian hates what God hates

A true believer hates evil because he is inextricably intertwined with God Himself, who is pure and holy. When Peter realized he had denied the Lord three times, "he went out, and wept bitterly" (Matt. 26:75). Such love for God rejects the evil of this world. That's why 1 John 2:15 says, "Love not the world, neither the things that are in the world. If any man love the world, the love of the Father is not in him."

i) A true Christian longs for Christ's return

Second Timothy 4:8 says a special crown awaits all those who long for Christ's return.

j) A true Christian obeys God's commands

Obedience is the most obvious mark of a true believer's love for God. Christ said, "He that hath my commandments, and keepeth them, he it is that loveth me" (John 14:21). Those who keep God's commandments truly love Him.

True Christians love God: their hearts' desire is to know Him, glorify Him, commune with Him, and obey Him. We don't obey as completely as we ought, but that's our desire. We identify with Paul, who said, "I delight in the law of God after the inward man" (Rom. 7:22). Show me a person who doesn't have those desires, and I'll show you a person who isn't redeemed. A believer loves God—even though at times he may fail Him.

Can an unbeliever generate that kind of love for God? No. Romans 3:10-11 tells us no one can do good on his own, no matter how hard he tries. Believers "have peace with God" (Rom. 5:1). Unbelievers, in contrast, are at war with God. A person who is at war with God—who is ignorant, in darkness, and hopeless—cannot love God on his own.

There are only two kinds of people in the world: those who love God and those who hate Him. Unregenerate people don't see themselves as haters of God, especially if they are religious, but that is in fact the case. They do not obey God's Word, and obedience is the overarching mark of genuine love for God. Those who love God keep His commandments, and those who hate God don't. Those who are Christians don't love God as much as they should, but their hearts' desire is to love and obey Him. How can people who are dead in sin—who hate God—ever be turned around to love God?

B. Those Who Are Called

God's call is what changes a person from a hater of God to a lover of God. Christians didn't decide one day to stop hatingg God and start loving Him. Our fallen human nature keeps us from doing that. By calling us, God made us into people who love Him. The apostle John said, "We love him, because he first loved us" (1 John 4:19). The identifying mark of a Christian is love for God, yet that love first came from God Himself.

1. The calling defined

Matthew 22:14 says, "Many are called, but few are chosen." That verse appears in a parable about people who are called to come to the Lord. Here the call is an external invitation: many people hear the gospel and are invited to respond to it. However, only a few are "chosen." That's an internal call from God. Matthew 7:14 confirms that not many people will be saved: "Narrow is the gate, and hard is the way, which leadeth unto life, and few there be that find it."

That internal call is God's moving into a person's heart and turning it around, bringing about redemption. In the epistles "called" refers only to what theologians term an effectual call, meaning those whom God calls He inevitably redeems.

a) Romans 8:30—"Whom he did predestinate, them he also called; and whom he called, them he also justified; and whom he justified, them he also glorified."

b) Romans 9:11—"The children being not yet born, neither having done any good or evil, that the purpose of God according to election might stand, not of works, but of him that calleth." Salvation originates from the effectual call of God—His divine purpose and choosing—not from anything we have done or will do.

You love God because He first loved you. You responded to the gospel because God changed your heart—He initiated your salvation. As Martyn-Lloyd Jones said, "God interferes with our life" (*Romans*, vol. 6 [Grand Rapids: Zondervan, 1975], p. 190). And He interferes with our life in a significant way: His divine act initiated our salvation and ultimately leads to our glorification.

2. The calling described

People frequently ask me if I believe in predestination. I do because the Bible teaches it. Election and predestination are both in Romans 8:29-30, which tells us we are saved because God called us.

Paul realized he was "called to be an apostle of Jesus Christ" (1 Cor. 1:1). He didn't come to Christ on his own. Quite the contrary, God ordained him into the ministry while he was an unbeliever traveling to Damascus to persecute Christians. Paul had little to do with his conversion; he simply obeyed what God told him to do. Paul wrote 1 Corinthians to "the church of God which is at Corinth, to them that are sanctified in Christ Jesus, called to be saints" (1:2). Verse 24 also refers to God's effectual call: "Unto them who are called, both Jews and Greeks, Christ [is] the power of God, and the wisdom of God."

If you are a Christian, it's because God called you. Don't ask me why He picked you; I don't know why He picked me, but I rejoice just the same.

We find many references to the internal call of God throughout the epistles:

a) Ephesians 1:11—"In [Christ] we have obtained an inheritance, being predestinated according to the purpose of him who worketh all things after the counsel of his own will."

b) Philippians 3:14—"I press toward the mark for the prize of the high calling of God in Christ Jesus." Paul was called to the race to run for the prize.

c) 1 Thessalonians 2:13—"When ye received the word of God which ye heard of us, ye received it, not as the word of men but as it is in truth, the word of God, which effectually worketh also in you that believe."

d) 2 Timothy 1:9—"[God] hath saved us, and called us with an holy calling, not according to our works, but according to his own purpose and grace, which was given us in Christ Jesus before the world began."

You and I were called before the world began. God called us in eternity past so He could glorify us in eternity future. That's why it's impossible to lose our salvation. Why do all things work together for good to those who love God? Because they are the "called; and whom he called, them he also justified; and whom he justified, them he also glorified" (Rom. 8:30). We have been called to glory. God predestined us "to be conformed to the image of his Son" (v. 29). We are not complete until we are like Christ. God is working that out now. Jesus said, "Those that thou [the Father] gavest me I have kept, and none of them is lost" (John 17:12). God planned salvation to be eternal.

How Does God Call Us?

God calls us by His Word and His Spirit. Romans 10:17 says, "Faith comes from hearing, and hearing by the word of Christ" (NASB). Can a person be called and saved without hearing about Christ? No. Some people believe a person can be saved without knowing it, a teaching known as hyper-Calvinism, but Scripture says saving faith requires hearing about Christ (Rom. 10:14). A person first has to know the facts. God also calls us by

131

His Spirit. We are born again by the Spirit (1 Pet. 1:22-23). The Spirit convicts us "of sin, and of righteousness, and of judgment" (John 16:8). He recreates us. We are baptized into the Body of Christ in Him (1 Cor. 12:13). The Spirit and the Word are the agents of God's call.

III.   THE SOURCE (v. 28d)

"According to his purpose."

You could never save yourself, and you could never keep yourself saved. God had to save you, and He has to keep you saved. He is our source of security. Ephesians 1:4 says, "He hath chosen us in him before the foundation of the world, that we should be holy and without blame." God chose us for ultimate holiness—that is the supreme guarantee of glory. He planned our glorification, and nothing can stand in the way of that.

How does God know whom to set His love upon? I don't know—that's something He predetermined before the world began. But let me tell you something wonderful: God will not change His mind. He will not reject you if you are already saved. Romans 11:29 says, "The gifts and calling of God are without repentance."

IV.   THE CERTAINTY (v. 28a)

"We know."

We who love God know that we have been called and that all things work together for our good because that's what Scripture tells us. It grieves me that so many Christians don't know what the Bible says and therefore fail to experience the incredible rest that belongs to those who know their salvation is eternal. Others quote Romans 8:28 as a fact, yet they aren't confident of its truth.

Conclusion

All things do work together for the good of those who love God and are called according to His purpose. The supreme illustration of that is the death of Jesus Christ. The worst thing that ever happened in human history turned out to be the best thing that could have happened to us. God works to overrule everything for our ultimate good and glory!

Focusing on the Facts

1. Can anything overrule God's plan to glorify us? Support your answer with Scripture (see p. 124).
2. Who are the recipients of the promise that "all things work together for good" (see p. 124)?
3. Exodus 20:6 divides all humanity into two groups. What are they (see p. 125)?
4. Why does Paul identify Christians as those who love God in Romans 8:28 (see p. 125)?
5. Explain what the Lord is saying in Luke 6:46 (see pp. 125-26).
6. What characterizes the believer's love for God (see pp. 126-28)?
7. What is the most obvious mark of a believer's love for God (see p. 128)?
8. Can an unbeliever initiate love for God on his own? Explain (see p. 129).
9. Explain the difference between an external call and an internal call (see p. 129).
10. What does Romans 9:11 point out about the call of God versus the effort of man (see p. 130)?
11. Explain how God calls us (see pp. 131-32).
12. Can a person be saved without knowing any facts about Christ (Rom. 10:14; see p. 131)?
13. Who is the source of our eternal security? When did God choose us to be saved (Eph. 1:4; see p. 132)?
14. What is the supreme illustration of the truth that "all things work together for good to them that love God" (see pp. 132-33)?

Pondering the Principles

1. The Bible identifies believers as those who love God. How would you rate your love for God? Do you express your love consistently, regardless of your circumstances? How do you express your love for Him? Be specific. What do your answers reveal about your love for God? Determine what you need to do to make your love for God more of what it should be.

133

2. Review the section on what characterizes the believer's love for God (pp. 126-28). Carefully consider each characteristic. Which are your strengths? Which do you need to work on? Determine how you can strengthen the ones you need to work on, and ask God to help you.

3. Read 1 Thessalonians 5:23-24; 2 Thessalonians 2:13-14; and 2 Timothy 1:9. What do these verses say about your calling in general? Now look up the following verses, and describe what you are called to specifically: 1 Corinthians 1:9; Galatians 5:13; Ephesians 4:1-3; Hebrews 9:15; 1 Peter 1:15; 2:9; and 3:9. Thank God for calling you to salvation and to all the other things you've been called to!

10

The Ultimate Security of Our Salvation

Outline

Introduction
A. The Confusion
B. The Clarification

Lesson
I. The Purpose of Salvation (v. 29c)
   A. To Conform Us to Christ
      1. Bodily conformity
      2. Spiritual conformity
   B. To Make Christ Preeminent
II. The Progress of Salvation (vv. 29a-b, 30)
   A. Foreknowledge (v. 29a)
   B. Predestination (vv. 29b, 30a)
   C. Calling (v. 30b)
   D. Justification (v. 30c)
   E. Glorification (v. 30d)

Conclusion

Introduction

A. The Confusion

For years people have debated whether a Christian can lose his or her salvation. Perhaps more than any other single doctrine, eternal security has been a dividing issue in the church. That's sad because the Bible is so clear on the matter. It's surprising that so many Christians would deny the straightforward presentation of the doctrine of security in Romans 8. Other texts discuss the security of the believer, but none are as pointed as this. Verses 28-30 are among the clearest passages on eternal security: everyone who has been redeemed by Jesus Christ—without exception—will be glorified. All believers have the assurance that everything works together for their good, so nothing can work against them that could make them lose their salvation. The justified will indeed be glorified.

B. The Clarification

1. In Romans

Romans 8:28 says we are forever secure because that is God's purpose. Verses 29-30 explain God's purpose: "Whom he did foreknow, he also did predestinate to be conformed to the image of his Son, that he might be the first-born among many brethren. Moreover, whom he did predestinate, them he also called; and whom he called, them he also justified; and whom he justified, them he also glorified."

God causes all things to work together for the believer's good because that's the way He wants it. There's no other explanation. God is absolutely free to make whatever decisions He wants to, and nothing can change that.

2. In Ephesians

You're a Christian not because of something you decided, but because of something *God* decided. Paul said, "He hath chosen us in him before the foundation of the world, that we should be holy and without blame before him" (Eph. 1:4). God chose us and "predestinated us unto the adoption of sons by Jesus Christ to himself, according to the good pleasure of his will" (v. 5). God predetermined to make us His sons and planned our salvation to lead to glorification. Our security depends not on our ability to stay saved but on God's ability to keep His promise (Heb. 6:17-18). John 1:12-13 says, "As many as received him [Christ], to them gave he power to become the children of God, even to them that believe on his name; who were born, not of blood, nor of the will of the flesh, nor of the will of man, but of God." We need to receive Christ, but it is God who originates the new birth.

Your Decision vs. God's Decision

Much of contemporary evangelism leaves people thinking their salvation is predicated on their decision for Christ. But how could anyone ever decide for God on his own? First Corinthians 2:14 says, "The natural man receiveth not the things of the Spirit of God; for they are foolishness unto him." Second Corinthians 4:4 says, "The god of this world hath blinded the minds of them who believe not, lest the light of the glorious gospel of Christ, who is the image of God, should shine unto them." Man is ignorant, in darkness, and dead in trespasses and sin (Eph. 2:1). In his natural state he could never muster up enough of whatever it takes to turn around and follow God. God must make the first move. He purposes to save us in eternity past and redeem us for eternity future. There is no loss of salvation in between. Our salvation is secure because it is something God has purposed to do.

Lesson

I. THE PURPOSE OF SALVATION (v. 29c)

"To be conformed to the image of his Son, that he might be the first-born [Gk., *prōtotokos*] among many brethren."

A. To Conform Us to Christ

We have been called according to God's purpose, and His purpose is to make us like Christ. It is impossible to become saved but never become like Christ. God promised glorification. Heaven, the forgiveness of sin, and the gifts of love, joy, peace, and wisdom are mere by-products of salvation. The main reason God saved us was to conform us to the image of His Son.

God is redeeming an eternally holy, Christlike, glorified community of people. When you became a Christian, the conforming process began. And that process must be fulfilled because it is God's holy purpose. Romans 8:17 says that because we are children of God, we are "heirs of God, and joint heirs with Christ." We were made sons of God so that we might be heirs, and our inheritance is to be like Christ and to inherit all that belongs to Him. The teaching that people can lose their salvation is unbiblical because God's purpose in salvation is to conform us to the image of Christ.

137

The Greek verb translated "to be conformed" in verse 9 means "to bring to the same form with." We will be made into the same form as Christ.

1. Bodily conformity

Philippians 3:21 says that the Lord "shall change our lowly body, that it may be fashioned like his glorious body." Our glorified bodies will be like Christ's glorified body. Outwardly we will be conformed to the postresurrection body of our Lord, but I don't think that means we will look alike. Every human being is different, but we have basically the same body. Our bodies work in the same way, in the same environment, and by the same principles. When we go to glory, we will receive glorious bodies that operate in the same environment and by the same principles as the resurrected, glorified body of Christ.

2. Spiritual conformity

We will be like Christ in a spiritual sense as well: we will be perfect inwardly, not just outwardly. Residing in us will be the very holiness of Jesus Christ. The divine, incorruptible nature He gave us at our redemption will be freed from our earthbound flesh. We shall "be delivered from the bondage of corruption into the glorious liberty of the children of God" (Rom. 8:21).

God predestined us to be conformed "to the image [eikōn] of his Son." An icon is a statue made to look like someone or something. The likeness is not incidental or accidental—it is a calculated, replicated image. Eikōn is used of a son who is the image of his father. It is used that way in Hebrews 1:3, which describes God's Son as "the express image of his person." We too will be a direct replication of His image, for when Christ appears, "we shall be like him; for we shall see him as he is" (1 John 3:2).

Paul said, "We all, with unveiled face beholding as in a mirror the glory of the Lord, are changed into the same image from glory to glory, even as by the Spirit of the Lord" (2 Cor. 3:18). When you came to Christ, your spiritual blindness ended and you began to see the glory of the Lord. Now as you move from one level of glory to the next, you are becoming more and more like Christ until the day you actually see Christ and become like Him.

B. To Make Christ Preeminent

Although our conformity to Christ is vital to God's purpose, it is but a secondary purpose leading to this: "That [Christ] might be the first-born [Gk., *prōtotokos*] among many brethren." That's a reference to preeminence, not chronology. In Jewish culture, the firstborn son inherited a double portion of all his father possessed. He uniquely represented the dignity of his family and carried the family name. He was the preeminent one. God saved us to make us like Christ so there will be a redeemed, glorified humanity over which Christ will reign supreme.

Philippians 2:9-10 says God has exalted Christ "and given him a name which is above every name, that at the name of Jesus every knee should bow." He wants to bring to heaven a redeemed humanity that will spend all eternity glorifying the *prōtotokos*—the preeminent Christ. Colossians 1:18 declares that Christ "is the head of the body, the church; who is the beginning, the first-born from the dead, that in all things he might have the pre-eminence."

Why Did God Create Us?

God created us so there would be a group of people who would give Him the glory He deserves. Once the rebellion began in the Garden of Eden, God set out to redeem humanity. His goal in salvation is to bring believers to glory—to create an eternally redeemed community of people like Christ, whom they will glorify, worship, revere, and praise forever.

God saved you not just to keep you out of hell or to make you happy. His ultimate reason is to conform you to Christ's image so you will be able to give glory to the One who is most glorious.

In Hebrews 2:11 Christ calls us brothers. Now He didn't have to make us His brothers. He could have made us His servants. He didn't have to bring us into His family, but He did. Even though God wants us to glorify Him and His Son, He also desires intimacy with us. He wants us to be one in essence with Himself.

God gives us joy, peace, and a future in heaven—all elements of His grace to sinners. Yet we must not let those blessings obscure the apex of the divine purpose. Christ is the central point of redemptive history, not you. That's humbling in one sense but reassuring in another: if God saved you, He will glorify you to fulfill His purpose in bringing you to salvation. God's plans don't get thwarted. If they did, He wouldn't be God.

II. THE PROGRESS OF SALVATION (vv. 29a-b, 30)

There are five elements in the unfolding plan of salvation.

A. Foreknowledge (v. 29a)

"Whom he did foreknow."

God's redemptive plan began with His foreknowledge.

1. It includes foresight

Some people assume foreknowledge is the same as foresight. They envision God in heaven looking into the future with binoculars to see who will choose to believe in Christ. If He sees you will believe, He chooses you; if He sees you won't, He doesn't. God does have foresight: He can see everything that will happen in the future. He knows exactly what people will do. However, if salvation is based only on God's foresight into the decisions of individual men and women, that means man secures his own salvation—an obvious contradiction of Scripture. Also, the foresight view, instead of solving problems, leaves us with a couple.

a) Why did God create unbelievers?

Just believing that God foresaw who would and would not accept Christ doesn't explain why God allows people to go to hell. Some will say it's His choice to send people to hell; He knows it's going to happen. But if God knew certain people would go to hell, why did He bother creating them?

b) How does a sinner obtain saving faith?

Although God does foresee what is going to happen in the future, that still doesn't explain how sinners get saving faith. How can a person who is dead in sin, blinded by Satan, unable to understand the things of God, and continuously filled with evil suddenly exercise saving faith? A corpse could sooner come out of a grave and walk!

2. It includes foreordination

God's foreknowledge is not a reference to His omniscient foresight but to His foreordination. God does foresee who is going to be a believer, but the faith He foresees is the faith He Himself creates. Jesus said, "All that the Father giveth me shall come to me. . . . No man can come to me, except the Father, who hath sent me, draw him" (John 6:37, 44). John 1:13 says Christians are "born, not of blood, nor of the will of the flesh, nor of the will of man, but of God." Ephesians 2:8-9 says, "By grace are ye saved through faith; and that not of yourselves, it [faith] is the gift of God—not of works, lest any man should boast." Saving faith comes from God.

Acts 13:48 says, "When the Gentiles heard . . . they were glad, and glorified the word of the Lord; and as many as were ordained to eternal life believed." Salvation is ordained of God. It ultimately ends in eternal life and glory and a person's being conformed to the image of Christ. The Gentiles in Acts 13 believed because they were ordained to do so.

God doesn't merely see what will happen in the future, but ordains what will happen. The Bible clearly teaches that God sovereignly chooses people to believe in Him. The epistle of 1 Peter begins, "Peter, an apostle of Jesus Christ, to the sojourners scattered throughout Pontus, Galatia, Cappadocia, Asia, and Bithynia, elect according to the foreknowledge of God, the Father" (vv. 1-2). We are elect by God's foreknowledge.

3. It includes forelove

God predetermined to love us. "Foreknow" (Gk., *prognōsis*) is the key word in Romans 8:29. The word *know* is often used in Scripture to speak of a love relationship. Genesis 4:17 says, "Cain knew his wife; and she conceived, and bore Enoch." That doesn't mean Cain knew who his wife was or what her name was; it means he knew her intimately. Joseph was surprised when Mary became pregnant with Jesus because he had not yet known her intimately (Matt. 1:18, 25). Jesus said, "My sheep hear my voice, and I know them" (John 10:27). God told Israel, "You only have I known" (Amos 3:2). He didn't mean He knew only about the Jewish people. According to Matthew 7:23 the Lord will someday say to unbelievers, "I never knew you; depart from me, ye that work iniquity." In that case there was no predetermined love relationship, as when a man knows his wife.

God's foreknowledge means He predetermined to love certain people. He foreordained the redemption of those people, and could foresee it all happening in the future. So foreknowledge is a predetermined, foreordained, foreseen love relationship. Romans 8:28 says we are "called according to his purpose." Before the world began God purposed to love us and redeem us so we might be conformed to Christ's image. Second Timothy 2:19 says, "The Lord knoweth them that are his." Christ knows us intimately.

B. Predestination (vv. 29b, 30a)

"He also did predestinate. . . . Moreover, whom he did predestinate."

The Greek word translated "predestinate" (proorizō) means "to appoint" or "mark out beforehand." In Acts 4:27-28 it speaks of Christ's crucifixion: "Against thy holy child, Jesus, whom thou has appointed, both Herod, and Pontius Pilate, with the nations, and the people of Israel, were gathered together, to do whatever thy hand and thy counsel determined before to be done." The word *foreknowledge* is also used in reference to Christ's crucifixion (Acts 2:23). If we say God's foreknowledge is simply foresight into the future, that means He saw what Jesus—on His own prerogative—was going to do and reacted to it. That is heretical. But if we understand foreknowledge and predestination to mean that God predetermined Christ's death to redeem mankind, then it follows He could also predetermine who would be redeemed.

C. Calling (v. 30b)

"Them he also called."

Here's where God's eternal plan intersects with your life. In eternity past, He predetermined to love you—He predestined your salvation. God's calling begins when He moves into your life on this earth, within the boundaries of time.

Romans 8:28 says, "All things work together for good to them that love God, to them who are the called." "Called" refers not to an outward but an inward call. God turns a person's heart to Himself—a heart that could never turn to God, know Him, understand the gospel, or know hope on its own. The context of Romans 8:30 shows God's call to be a saving call: "Whom he called, them he also justified." And that calling is an effectual or effective call—it's not an invitation to just anyone, and it's an invitation that will inevitably be received. Since God predetermined to love us, foreordaining our salvation in eternity past, He has to fulfill that by moving into our lives.

When God calls us, He convicts our hearts. He draws us away from sin and toward the Savior. Paul said, "[God] hath saved us, and called us with an holy calling, not according to our works, but according to his own purpose and grace, which was given us in Christ Jesus before the world began" (2 Tim. 1:9). You were called to salvation to fulfill a purpose that was planned before the world began. That's why we are secure in our salvation. We were saved to be like Christ as part of a redeemed community that will exalt His holy name forever. Since that was God's plan before we were born, He will fulfill it, working out all things toward that good end.

1. Through the gospel

God's call comes to us through the gospel. Paul said, "We are bound to give thanks always to God for you, brethren beloved of the Lord, because God hath from the beginning chosen you to salvation . . . unto which he called you by our gospel, to the obtaining of the glory of our Lord Jesus Christ" (2 Thess. 2:13-14).

Perplexing Paradoxes

Contemporary Christianity has a shallow view of salvation. Many people don't understand the security of the believer. God, in eternity past, chose us to believe in the truth (2 Thess. 2:13). But there must be a response on our part. Now I don't fully understand how those two come together. Does that mean people go to hell because God didn't choose them? No. The

Bible says they go to hell because they reject the gospel (John 3:18).

The paradox of God's choice and man's response isn't the only paradox in Scripture. For example, who wrote the book of Romans? Paul did, and so did God. Every word is pure and from the mind of God. Yet every word is also from Paul's heart and his vocabulary. How could Romans have been fully written by both God and Paul? We know it was but can't fully explain it. Is Jesus God or man? He was both. Christ was not a blend of God and man. He was 200 percent Himself: 100 percent God and 100 percent man. Who lives your Christian life? Paul said, "I keep under my body, and bring it into subjection" (1 Cor. 9:27). He also said, "I am crucified with Christ: nevertheless I live; yet not I, but Christ liveth in me" (Gal. 2:20). Which is the right answer? Both you and Christ live your life.

Most major doctrines in the Bible have aspects we cannot fully explain. When we attempt to bring God down to our level, there is still much we won't understand. Let's go back to our original question: Why do people go to hell? If a person rejects Christ, he's responsible. But if a person comes to Christ, that means he was chosen in Christ before the foundation of the world (Eph. 1:4). There's no other explanation.

2. By grace

God's call to Christ also comes by grace. Don't think you must be better just because God chose you. We don't know why God chose you or me. One small hint appears in Ephesians 1:6, which says God predestined us "to the praise of the glory of his grace." Whatever the reason, God chose us for Himself. Galatians 1:6 says He calls us "into the grace of Christ." We are called to salvation through the gospel and by grace.

D. Justification (v. 30c)

"Whom he called, them he also justified."

The Greek word translated "justified" means "to be made right." How do you get right with God? When you deal with the sin in your life. How does that happen? When God takes your sin and puts it on Christ (Rom. 3:23-25). When God moved into your heart and called you to faith in Christ, you became right with God.

Is there time between God's calling and our justification? I don't know. That's like asking how much time it takes for a bullet to go through two sheets of paper. The distinction between calling and justification is theological; there isn't necessarily a time lapse. You are called to be justified. The calling takes place when God moves to change your heart. Justification is the result.

E. Glorification (v. 30*d*)

"Whom he justified, them he also glorified."

That passage is in the past tense. Your glorification is so secure that God speaks of it as if it already happened, as did your calling and justification. In one great moment of eternal time, God determined that all those things would happen to you. The moment He predetermined to love you, the outcome of your salvation was just as sure as its beginning.

Conclusion

You were saved unto glory, and all things are working toward that end. God's purpose is to make you like Christ as part of a redeemed humanity over which Christ will be preeminent. You will glorify and praise Him forever. Before the world began, God predetermined to love you and foreordain your salvation. In time He moved into your heart and called you away from your sin. He made you right with Himself through Jesus Christ, and destined you to be glorified. That is the great basis of your eternal security.

Focusing on the Facts

1. What doctrine, perhaps more than any other, has been a dividing issue in the church? Why is that surprising (see p. 135-36)?
2. How do we know believers are secure forever (Rom. 8:28; see p. 136)?
3. When did God choose us (Eph. 1:4; see p. 136)?
4. What does our security depend on? Explain (Heb. 6:17-18; see p. 136).
5. What do many think salvation is predicated on? Respond to that belief biblically (see p. 137).

6. In what ways will we be conformed to Christ? Discuss what is involved in each aspect of transformation (see p. 138).

7. What is the significance of the word "image" in Romans 8:29 (see p. 138)?

8. What does it mean that Christ is "the first-born among many brethren" (Rom. 8:29; see p. 139)?

9. What do some people suggest about God's foreknowledge? What problems are we left with (see pp. 140-41)?

10. Where does the faith God foresees come from (see p. 141)?

11. Using Scripture, support the fact that God sovereignly ordains people to salvation (see p. 141).

12. What is *know* often used to speak of in Scripture, and how does that relate to God's love for us (see pp. 141-42)?

13. What does the Greek word translated "predestinate" mean (Rom. 8:29-30; see p. 142)?

14. What happens when God calls us? How does His call come to us (see pp. 142-44)?

15. What hint does Ephesians 1:6 give about why God chose to save us (see p. 144)?

16. What does it mean to be justified (Rom. 8:30)? Discuss the relationship between God's call and justification (see pp. 144-45).

17. Explain why Romans 8:30 describes believers as already glorified (see p. 145).

Pondering the Principles

1. One aspect of God's purpose for salvation is to create an eternally redeemed humanity that will glorify Christ forever. Why is Christ worthy of glory? How often do you focus on glorifying Him? Make a list of things you can praise Him for, and lift them up to Him in prayer.

2. Romans 8:30 says that those whom God justified He also glorified. Our salvation is as good as done. We can definitely trust God for our eternal security. Do you have that same kind of trust in God for the temporal things of day-to-day life? In what ways do you show a lack of confidence in God? Do you, for instance, tend to worry? What are you telling God when you don't trust Him fully? Cultivate a habit of trusting God in every aspect of your life. Since He can guarantee your future glorification, He certainly can take care of you in your present circumstances.

11

The Hymn of Security—Part 1

Outline

Introduction

Lesson
I. No One Can Revoke Our Salvation (vv. 31-34)
   A. We Are Secure in God (vv. 31-32)
      1. He protects us (v. 31)
      2. He loves us (v. 32)
         a) By giving His Son (v. 32a)
         b) By giving every spiritual blessing (v. 32b)
   B. We Are Secure Against Satan (v. 33)
   C. We Are Secure in Christ (v. 34)
      1. Because of His death (v. 34a)
      2. Because of His resurrection (v. 34b)
      3. Because of His exaltation (v. 34c)
      4. Because of His intercession (v. 34d)

Introduction

Romans 8:31-39 says, "What shall we then say to these things? If God be for us, who can be against us? He that spared not his own Son, but delivered him up for us all, how shall he not with him also freely give us all things? Who shall lay any thing to the charge of God's elect? Shall God that justifieth? Who is he that condemneth? Shall Christ that died, yea rather, that is risen again, who is even at the right hand of God, who also maketh intercession for us?

"What shall separate us from the love of Christ? Shall tribulation, or distress, or persecution, or famine, or nakedness, or

147

peril, or sword? As it is written, For thy sake we are killed all the day long; we are accounted as sheep for the slaughter. Nay, in all these things we are more than conquerors through him that loved us.

"For I am persuaded that neither death, nor life, nor angels, nor principalities, nor powers, nor things present, nor things to come, nor height, nor depth, nor any other creation, shall be able to separate us from the love of God, which is in Christ Jesus, our Lord."

In verse 31 "these things" refers to the truths about eternal security. Paul then proceeds from there to the end of the chapter to show that neither people nor circumstances—no one or nothing—can revoke the believer's salvation.

Lesson

I. NO ONE CAN REVOKE OUR SALVATION (vv. 31-34)

A. We Are Secure in God (vv. 31-32)

"What shall we then say to these things? If God be for us, who can be against us? He that spared not his own Son, but delivered him up for us all, how shall he not with him also freely give us all things?"

A believer might say, "God can take back my salvation." But that's not true since God both protects and loves the believer.

1. He protects us (v. 31)

Since the Greek term translated "if" (*ei*) refers to the fulfillment of something, verse 31 is better translated, "Since God is for us, who can be against us?" God protects us from all who would seek to pull us away from the salvation He offers.

a) Luke 22:31-32—Christ said to Peter, "Simon, Simon, behold, Satan hath desired to have you, that he may sift you as wheat. But I have prayed for thee, that thy faith fail not. And when thou art converted, strengthen thy brethren." Not even the highest of the fallen angels can wrest the believer from Christ (cf. John 10:28-29).

148

b) Psalm 27:1-3, 6—David said, "The Lord is my light and my salvation; whom shall I fear? The Lord is the strength of my life; of whom shall I be afraid? When the wicked, even mine enemies and my foes, came upon me to eat up my flesh, they stumbled and fell. Though an host should encamp against me, my heart shall not fear; though war should rise against me, in this will I be confident. . . .

"And now shall mine head be lifted up above mine enemies round about me. Therefore will I offer in his tabernacle sacrifices of joy; I will sing, yea, I will sing praises unto the Lord." Because of God's protection, David did not fear the serious opposition he faced.

c) Psalm 46:1-3—"God is our refuge and strength, a very present help in trouble. Therefore will not we fear, though the earth be removed, and though the mountains be carried into the midst of the sea; though the waters thereof roar and be troubled, though the mountains shake with the swelling thereof." David was secure in the Lord's strength.

2. He loves us (v. 32)

a) By giving His Son (v. 32*a*)

"He that spared not his own Son, but delivered him up for us all."

A believer might say, "God will protect me as long as He's for me. But if He thinks I'm not good, He might reject me." Paul countered that objection by pointing out that since God gave His Son to die for us when we were sinners, He certainly will keep us now that we're His children. God willingly gave His Son to die on our behalf because He loves us (John 3:16). Taking back our salvation would defy His love and undo His redemptive work.

A Human Picture of God's Love

Just as God willingly offered His Son, so Abraham was willing to offer his son Isaac. As Abraham was just about to do so, the Lord said to him, "Lay not thine hand upon the lad, neither do thou anything unto him; for now I know that thou fearest God, seeing thou hast not withheld thy son, thine only son from me. . . . By myself have I sworn, saith the Lord; for because thou hast done this thing, and hast not withheld thy son, thine only son; that in blessing I will bless thee" (Gen. 22:12, 16-17). As a progenitor of Christ, blessing and salvation would come through him to all the nations of the earth.

In Romans 8:32 the Greek term translated "own" (*idios*) emphasizes the Father's intimate, private possession of His Son. Although the Father did not have to give His Son to die on the cross, He chose to do so. Isaiah 53:10 says, "It pleased the Lord to bruise him." Second Corinthians 5:21 says God "hath made him, who knew no sin, to be sin for us."

God willingly gave His Son "for us all" (Rom. 8:32), which means He died for our benefit and in our place. "Us" refers to believers (v. 28). Galatians 3:13 says, "Christ hath redeemed us from the curse of the law, being made a curse for us." Galatians 1:4 says that Christ "gave himself for our sins."

b) By giving every spiritual blessing (v. 32*b*)

"How shall he not with him also freely give us all things?"

"All things" refer to all spiritual blessings, including eternal glory. Since the Father willingly gave His Son to die on the cross, He certainly won't hold back on the fruits of that atoning work. Indeed, He "hath blessed us with all spiritual blessings in heavenly places in Christ" (Eph. 1:3).

Sometimes "give" (Gk., *charizomai*) is translated "forgive" in the New Testament (e.g., Col. 2:13; 3:13). That would make the verse say, "God freely forgives all sins." Although one can't be dogmatic about that interpretation, the concept is nevertheless true. As 1 John 1:9 says, "If we confess our sins, he is faithful and just to forgive us our sins, and to cleanse us from all unrighteousness."

B. We Are Secure Against Satan (v. 33)

"Who shall lay any thing to the charge of God's elect? Shall God that justifieth?"

"Lay any thing to the charge" refers to bringing a legal charge against someone. No accusation before God's tribunal will cause the believer to lose his salvation. Revelation 12:10 says Satan constantly accuses believers before God. In Zechariah 3:1 we see Satan accusing Joshua the high priest. But the Lord rebuked Satan and protected Joshua (v. 2).

Our salvation is secure because God won't condemn the very person He has already justified (Rom. 8:1). Romans 4:20-25 tells us Christ's righteousness is imputed to us when we believe in Christ. That can't be taken back. What's more, our salvation doesn't depend on our goodness (Eph. 2:8-9).

"God's elect" (v. 33) refers to those whom He chose for salvation before the foundation of the world. Commentator Marcus Loane wrote, "Those who stand at the bar are not outlaws, but God's elect" (*The Hope of Glory* [Waco, Tex.: Word, 1968], p. 136). Since we are not on trial, we have nothing to fear at God's tribunal. Our salvation is secure in His election, for Christ said, "My Father, who gave them to me, is greater than all, and no man is able to pluck them out of my Father's hand" (John 10:29).

C. We Are Secure in Christ (v. 34)

"Who is he that condemneth? Shall Christ that died, yea rather, that is risen again, who is even at the right hand of God, who also maketh intercession for us?"

Christ won't ever condemn believers. John 3:17-18 says, "God sent not his Son into the world to condemn the world, but that the world through him might be saved. He that believeth on him is not condemned; but he that believeth not is condemned already because he hath not believed."

There are four reasons we are secure in Christ.

1. Because of His death (v. 34a)

"Shall Christ that died."

Since Christ bore the penalty for our sins, we are free from His condemnation when we acknowledge His death on our behalf. If we could still be condemned in spite of our faith in Christ, that would mean His death was inadequate to atone for our sins. But His death is more than sufficient; it is the only condemnation the believer will ever know.

2. Because of His resurrection (v. 34b)

"Yea rather, that is risen again."

The Greek term translated "yea rather" (*mallon*) can be translated "what is more." Christ's resurrection proves the sufficiency of His death in atoning for our sins. Romans 4:25 says Christ "was delivered for our offenses, and was raised again for our justification." His death paid the price for our sins, and His resurrection was proof of God's acceptance of that payment.

3. Because of His exaltation (v. 34c)

"Who is even at the right hand of God."

God's right hand is the place of exaltation and honor. Hebrews 1:3 says that when Christ purged our sins, He "sat down on the right hand of the Majesty on high" (cf. Ps. 110:1). The high priests of Israel had to stand each day and offer sacrifices again and again. But Christ offered one sacrifice for sins forever and then sat down at God's right hand (Heb. 10:11-12).

4. Because of His intercession (v. 34d)

"Who also maketh intercession for us?"

Our salvation is secure because Christ constantly intercedes for us.

a) Isaiah 53:12—Christ "made intercession for the transgressors."

b) 1 John 2:1—"We have an advocate with the Father, Jesus Christ the righteous."

152

c) Hebrews 7:25—Christ "is able also to save them to the uttermost that come unto God by him, seeing he ever liveth to make intercession for them."

Whenever we sin or Satan accuses us, Christ acts as our divine defense attorney by interceding on our behalf. He prays for us according to the Father's will, and the Father always responds.

Focusing on the Facts

1. What do "these things" refer to in Romans 8:31 (see p. 148)?
2. What is a better translation for "if" in verse 31, and what does that communicate (see p. 148)?
3. What was the Father's motive in giving His Son (John 3:16; see p. 149)?
4. What does "for us all" mean in Romans 8:32 (see p. 150)?
5. Galatians 1:4 says that "Christ gave _____ for our sins" (see p. 150).
6. What do "all things" refer to in Romans 8:32 (see p. 150)?
7. Who constantly accuses believers before God (Rev. 12:10; see p. 151)?
8. What does Romans 8:1 teach (see p. 151)?
9. What does Romans 4:20-25 tell us (see p. 151)?
10. What does Ephesians 2:8-9 teach (see p. 151)?
11. Who are "God's elect" (Rom. 8:33; see p. 151)?
12. What does John 3:17-18 teach (see p. 151)?
13. Christ's _____ proves the sufficiency of His death in atoning for our sins (see p. 152).
14. Romans 4:25 says Christ was delivered for our _____, and raised for our _____ (see p. 152).
15. What does Hebrews 10:11-12 tell us (see p. 152)?
16. Whenever we sin or Satan accuses us, how does Christ help us (Rom. 8:34; see pp. 152-53)?

Pondering the Principles

1. Answer the following questions:

    * Why did Christ die (1 Cor. 15:3; 1 Pet. 2:24; 3:18)?

    * According to Galatians 4:5 what does the believer receive?

    * What does Hebrews 10:10-14 say about Christ's death?

    * What does 1 Peter 1:3-5 teach about eternal security?

    * What does Hebrews 7:25 teach about Christ?

    Meditate on those verses, and thank the Lord for the eternal security of your salvation.

2. Suppose a believer says to you, "I fear I can lose my salvation." Use what you have learned in Romans 8:31-34 as your basis for clearing up that misunderstanding.

12

The Hymn of Security—Part 2

Outline

Introduction

Review
I. No One Can Revoke Our Salvation (vv. 31-34)
    A. We Are Secure in God (vv. 31-32)
    B. We Are Secure Against Satan (v. 33)
    C. We Are Secure in Christ (v. 34)

Lesson
II. Nothing Can Revoke Our Salvation (vv. 35-39)
    A. Our Adversities (v. 35)
        1. Pressure
        2. Temptation
        3. Suffering
        4. Hunger
        5. Poverty
        6. Danger
        7. Death
    B. Our Perseverance (v. 36)
    C. Our Victory (v. 37)
    D. Our Confidence (vv. 38-39)
        1. We are secure against death
        2. We are secure in life
        3. We are secure against angels
        4. We are secure against demons
        5. We are secure for both time and eternity
        6. We are secure against everything in the celestial realm
        7. We are secure against everyone and everything

Conclusion

Introduction

In Jeremiah 31:3 God says to the Israelites, "I have loved thee with an everlasting love." As the object of God's love, the apostle Paul could say, "I know whom I have believed and am persuaded that he is able to keep that which I have committed unto him against that day" (2 Tim. 1:12). In Romans 8:35-39 Paul declares that all true believers are the objects of God's love. Because that is so, neither people nor circumstances—no one or nothing—can revoke our salvation.

Review

I. NO ONE CAN REVOKE OUR SALVATION (vv. 31-34; see pp. 148-53)

A. We Are Secure in God (vv. 31-32; see pp. 148-50)

1. He protects us (v. 31)

    a) 1 John 4:4—"Greater is he that is in you, than he that is in the world." Because of God's greatness, we are secure in Him.

    b) Hebrews 13:6—Any believer can say, "I will not fear what man shall do unto me."

    c) Psalm 4:8; 56:3—David said, "I will both lie down in peace, and sleep; for thou, Lord, only makest me dwell in safety. . . . When I am afraid, I will trust in thee."

    d) Deuteronomy 33:27—Moses said, "The eternal God is thy refuge, and underneath are the everlasting arms."

    e) Psalm 91:1-2—David said, "He who dwelleth in the secret place of the Most High shall abide under the shadow [protection] of the Almighty. I will say of the Lord, he is my refuge and my fortress, my God; in him will I trust."

    f) Deuteronomy 33:29—"Happy art thou, O Israel! Who is like unto thee, O people saved by the Lord,

the shield of thy help, and who is the sword of thy
excellency?"

2. He loves us (v. 32)

   a) By giving His Son (v. 32a)

   To deny the believer's security is to misunderstand
   the heart of God, the gift of Christ, the meaning of
   the cross, and the biblical definition of salvation.
   Romans 5:8-10 says, "God commendeth his love
   toward us in that, while we were yet sinners,
   Christ died for us. Much more then, being now
   justified by his blood, we shall be saved from
   wrath through him. For if, when we were enemies,
   we were reconciled to God by the death of his Son,
   much more, being reconciled, we shall be saved by
   his life."

   b) By giving every spiritual blessing (v. 32b)

   God blesses us by supplying our every need (Phil.
   4:19). A person's greatest need is salvation, which
   includes glorification. Even when we sin, God's
   grace abounds toward us (Rom. 5:20-21; 2 Cor. 9:8).

B. We Are Secure Against Satan (v. 33; see p. 151)

No accusations before God's tribunal will cause Him to
revoke our salvation. The prophet Isaiah said, "He is near
who justifieth me. Who will contend with me? Let us
stand together. Who is mine adversary? Let him come
near to me. Behold, the Lord God will help me. Who is
he that shall condemn me?" (Isa. 50:8-9).

C. We Are Secure in Christ (v. 34; see pp. 151-53)

1. Because of His death (v. 34a)

   Christ won't revoke our salvation, because He died for
   us. Hebrews 9:14 says, "How much more shall the
   blood of Christ, who through the eternal Spirit offered
   himself without spot to God, purge your conscience
   from dead works to serve the living God?" Christ, the
   perfect High Priest, offered the perfect sacrifice, which
   gives us perfect standing before God. To deny our
   security is to deny the sufficiency of His atoning work.

2. Because of His resurrection (v. 34*b*)

3. Because of His exaltation (v. 34*c*)

4. Because of His intercession (v. 34*d*)

Lesson

II. NOTHING CAN REVOKE OUR SECURITY (vv. 35-39)

"What shall separate us from the love of Christ? Shall tribulation, or distress, or persecution, or famine, or nakedness, or peril, or sword? As it is written, For thy sake we are killed all the day long; we are accounted as sheep for the slaughter. Nay, in all these things we are more than conquerors through him that loved us. For I am persuaded that neither death, nor life, nor angels, nor principalities, nor powers, nor things present, nor things to come, nor height, nor depth, nor any other creation, shall be able to separate us from the love of God, which is in Christ Jesus, our Lord."

A. Our Adversities (v. 35)

"What shall separate us from the love of Christ? Shall tribulation, or distress, or persecution, or famine, or nakedness, or peril, or sword?"

In verse 33 the Greek term *tis* is translated "who," but in verse 35 it's translated "what." That's because the former deals with people and the latter with circumstances. "The love of Christ" (v. 35) refers to Christ's love for the believer, not that of the believer for Christ. Paul was asking, "What can make Christ stop loving you?" The implied answer: Nothing.

First John 4:19 says we love God because He first loved us. John 13:1 says that Christ, "having loved his own who were in the world, he loved them unto the end." Second Thessalonians 2:16-17 says, "Now our Lord Jesus Christ himself, and God, even our Father, who hath loved us, and hath given us everlasting consolation and good hope through grace, comfort your hearts, and establish you in every good word and work."

In Romans 8 Paul specifies various adversities that the believer might experience. Not one can separate the believer from Christ's love.

1. Pressure

In Romans 8:35 the Greek term translated "tribulation" (*thlipsis*) speaks of pressure from external difficulties. That includes suffering from false accusations, rejection, or bodily harm. Not even severe pressure can separate us from Christ's love.

2. Temptation

"Distress" (Gk., *stenochoria*) refers to internal pressure. It literally means "narrowness of room" and pictures someone who is caught in a narrow space or hemmed in with no way out in sight. I believe it's a specific reference to temptation. First Corinthians 10:13 says that when we face temptation, God will enable us to endure it and provide an eventual way out. Not even strong, internal temptations can separate us from Christ's love.

3. Suffering

"Persecution" (Gk., *diōgmos*) refers to physical or mental suffering at the hands of those who reject Christ. No such suffering can separate us from Christ's love.

4. Hunger

Can going without food, even to the point of starvation, separate us from Christ's love? Never.

5. Poverty

Can a lack of clothing or shelter separate us from Christ's love? Not at all.

6. Danger

"Peril" speaks of danger. Enemies were always plotting against Paul, so he was especially relieved to know that danger could never separate the believer from Christ's love.

7. Death

The Greek term translated "sword" (Gk., *machaira*) refers to an assassin's dagger. Not even imminent death can separate us from Christ's love.

Paul experienced much adversity in serving Christ: "Of the Jews five times received I forty stripes, save one. Thrice was I beaten with rods, once was I stoned, thrice I suffered shipwreck, a night and a day I have been in the deep; in journeyings often, in perils of waters, in perils of robbers, in perils by mine own countrymen, in perils by the Gentiles, in perils in the city, in perils in the wilderness, in perils in the sea, in perils among false brethren; in weariness and painfulness, in watchings often, in hunger and thirst, in fastings often, in cold and nakedness" (2 Cor. 11:24-27). Those trials never broke the bond of Christ's love for Paul, and no adversity will ever separate us from Christ's love either.

B. Our Perseverance (v. 36)

"As it is written, For thy sake we are killed all the day long; we are accounted as sheep for the slaughter."

That is a quotation of Psalm 44:22 from the Septuagint (the Greek translation of the Old Testament). Adversity has been the lot of God's people through all generations, so it's no surprise that we encounter it. Rather than breaking us away from God's love, it shows that we are part of God's family. Second Timothy 3:12 declares, "All that will live godly in Christ Jesus shall suffer persecution."

"For thy sake" in Romans 8:36 implies a willingness to endure adversity. First John 2:19 says all true believers will remain loyal to Christ. They will deny themselves, take up their cross, and follow Christ (Matt. 16:24). Hebrews 3:14 says, "We are made partakers of Christ, if we hold the beginning of our confidence steadfast unto the end." Christ said, "If ye continue in my word, then are ye my disciples indeed" (John 8:31). Perseverance during adversity is the mark of a true believer. He or she will be willing even to die for Christ's sake if necessary.

C. Our Victory (v. 37)

"Nay, in all these things we are more than conquerors through him that loved us."

The Greek term translated "more than conquerors" (*hupernikaō*) refers to an overwhelming victory. With Christ's help, we triumph over all adverse circumstances. That's because adversity refines us by increasing our love for righteousness and our hatred of sin. We see not only our own inadequacy but also Christ's sufficiency for every situation, confident "that all things work together for good to them that love God, to them who are the called according to his purpose" (Rom. 8:28).

Adversity works for us "a far more exceeding and eternal weight of glory" (2 Cor. 4:17). The refining process makes us recipients of a great reward in heaven. In the meantime, God grants us His grace through the Spirit of glory, who rests on us (1 Pet. 4:14).

Safe in the Arms of the Savior

Many believers in Rome surely began to wonder about the security of their salvation when people began leaving the church because of persecution. But rather than draw the true believer away from Christ, persecution instead reveals the genuineness of his or her faith (cf. Matt. 13:5-6, 20-21). The blood of believers soaked the sands of the Roman coliseum. Some Christians were mauled by wild beasts; others were soaked in tar and used as human torches for lighting Emperor Nero's night parties. Yet they faced death singing praises to Christ, knowing they were safe in the loving arms of their Savior.

D. Our Confidence (vv. 38-39)

"I am persuaded that neither death, nor life, nor angels, nor principalities, nor powers, nor things present, nor things to come, nor height, nor depth, nor any other creation, shall be able to separate us from the love of God, which is in Christ Jesus, our Lord."

That's Paul's capstone to the theme of justification by grace through faith. It's as though he were taking a paintbrush to enhance an already beautiful picture. "I am persuaded" speaks of a confident declaration or settled

161

conclusion. Paul expresses that same kind of confidence in 2 Timothy 1:12: "I know whom I have believed and am persuaded that he is able to keep that which I have committed unto him." Along with Paul, we are confident that nothing can separate us from God's love.

1. We are secure against death

   Death can't separate us from God's love. Psalm 116:15 says, "Precious in the sight of the Lord is the death of his saints." The Lord is with us as we walk through the valley of the shadow of death (Ps. 23:4).

Death Is Only a Shadow

When his wife died, minister Donald Grey Barnhouse tried to find a good way to explain the situation to his young children. As he was driving home from the funeral, a truck passed his car, casting a shadow over it. He asked his children, "Would you rather be run over by a truck or the shadow of a truck?" They answered, "The shadow because it doesn't hurt you." He said, "Mommy went through the valley of the shadow of death. There is no pain there." Instead of separating us from Christ, death will bring us into His presence (cf. 2 Cor. 5:8).

2. We are secure in life

   Life—in spite of all its dangers, difficulties, temptations, and troubles—cannot separate us from God's love (cf. Rom. 14:7-9).

3. We are secure against angels

   Paul was probably making a hypothetical reference to good angels. Galatians 1:8 says, "Though we, or an angel from heaven, preach any other gospel unto you than that which we have preached unto you, let him be accursed." A good angel can't separate us from God's love.

4. We are secure against demons

   Although "principalities" (Gk., archē) refers to both good and fallen angels in the New Testament, here it probably refers to the latter (cf. Eph. 6:12). No demon can separate us from God's love, neither can any of their "powers" (Gk., *dunamis*)—often a reference to miracles or mighty deeds.

5. We are secure for both time and eternity

"Things present" and "things future" mean that nothing in this age, future ages, or eternity can separate us from God's love.

6. We are secure against everything in the celestial realm

The Greek terms translated "height" (*hupsōma*) and "depth" (*bathos*) are astronomical terms. The former refers to the location of a star at its zenith, and the latter to its nadir. Nothing in all the celestial expanse can separate us from God's love.

7. We are secure against everyone and everything

"Any other creation" brings us back to our original outline: no one or nothing can separate us from God's love. Paul allowed no loopholes or exceptions. Even the believer can't separate himself from God's love.

Conclusion

"The love of God, which is in Christ Jesus, our Lord" (Rom. 8:39) means that the Father and Son's love are inseparable. Christ said it like this: "I in them, and thou in me, that they may be made perfect in one; and that the world may know that thou hast sent me, and hast loved them, as thou hast loved me. Father, I will that they also, whom thou hast given me, be with me where I am, that they may behold my glory, which thou hast given me; for thou lovedst me before the foundation of the world" (John 17:23-24). Christ prayed that His disciples might be with Him in heaven. Because God hears and answers that prayer, our salvation is eternally secure.

Focusing on the Facts

1. What does "the love of Christ" refer to in Romans 8:35 (see p. 158)?
2. What does 1 John 4:19 tell us (see p. 158)?

3. What is "distress" a specific reference to (Rom. 8:35; see p. 159)?
4. What does 2 Corinthians 11:24-27 tell us about Paul's experience in serving Christ (see p. 160)?
5. Why should it be no surprise to encounter adversity (see p. 160)?
6. Rather than breaking us away from God's love, what does adversity show us (see p. 160)?
7. What does "for thy sake" imply (Rom. 8:36; see p. 160)?
8. According to Matthew 16:24 how is the true believer to respond to adversity (see p. 160)?
9. What does "more than conquerors" refer to (Rom. 8:37; see p. 161)?
10. How does adversity refine us (see p. 161)?
11. Adversity works for us "a far more exceeding and eternal weight of _____" (2 Cor. 4:17; see p. 161).
12. What does adversity reveal (Matt. 13:20-21; see p. 161)?
13. What verses are the capstone to Paul's theme of justification by grace through faith (see p. 161)?
14. What do "things present" and "things future" mean (Rom. 8:38; see p. 163)?
15. What does "any other creation" bring us back to (Rom. 8:38; see p. 163)?
16. What does John 17:23-24 teach (see p. 163)?

Pondering the Principles

1. God's Word says that the believer is secure in God's arms, and will someday be glorified in heaven. What effect should that have on your behavior and your thoughts about God? Get together with your family or a Christian friend and share your answers to that question.

2. Are you encountering any difficult circumstances in your life right now? In light of Romans 8:35-39 what perspective should you have regarding your situation? Does that perspective apply to every situation you might encounter? As a Christian, you have every reason to be optimistic. Don't allow adversity to obscure God's promise that all things will ultimately work out for your good.

3. Meditate on Romans 8:38-39 and commit it to memory. Doing so will help bring joy and hope to your life.

Scripture Index

169

Topical Index